FLORIDA LITERARY LUMINARIES

WRITING IN PARADISE

JAMES C. CLARK

THE
History
PRESS

Published by The History Press
Charleston, SC
www.historypress.com

First published 2022

Manufactured in the United States

ISBN 9781467149792

Library of Congress Control Number: 2022931439

Notice: The information in this book is true and complete to the best of our knowledge. It is offered without guarantee on the part of the author or The History Press. The author and The History Press disclaim all liability in connection with the use of this book.

CONTENTS

CONTENTS

CONTENTS

ACKNOWLEDGEMENTS

For five hundred years, people have been writing about Florida and in Florida. This book features a broad selection of the authors, but for every author who is included there are five who are not. As always, I appreciate the work of the Florida Archives and Katelyn Herring and Adam Watson. Laureen Crowley once again tackled the daunting task of editing with good humor and great skill. Finally, my editor at The History Press, Joe Gartrell, has once again come through with his combination of sage advice, great patience and gentle nudging. Thanks to all.

THE FIRST CHAPTER

CABEZA DE VACA

Nearly half a century before the Pilgrims landed in New England or the Jamestown settlers came to Virginia, a small library of poems and books had been written about the Spanish in Florida.

The adventure of Cabeza de Vaca provided the first look at the interior of the continent. His story became one of the first major accounts of life in North America.

In early 1527, de Vaca sailed from Spain as part of an expedition of six hundred men with plans to settle on the Gulf Coast of Florida. Even before they reached Florida, however, they lost nearly a third of their number to storms and desertion.

When they landed near Tampa Bay, the men began arguing. Some thought there was gold to be found and wanted to search for it. Others wanted to stay with the ships on the coast in case of Indian attacks. The Indians did attack, and only 242 survivors reached Apalachee Bay in the Florida Panhandle. They planned to reconnect with the ship that brought them from Spain but never found it.

De Vaca thought he could find Spanish soldiers in Mexico, and he and his men decided to sail across the Gulf. They built five boats, each able to hold fifty men, and set sail heading west. A violent storm—probably a hurricane—separated the flotilla; only two ships and forty men survived, coming ashore near present-day Galveston. The survivors were enslaved by the Indians, and only four men from the original expedition reached Mexico City.

De Vaca sailed back to Europe, where he wrote his story, the first book devoted entirely to North America. Because he wrote from memory and was never sure exactly where he had been, his memoirs are full of geographical errors. His book, *La relación*, offered the first account of the Indians of North America. He was sympathetic toward the indigenous people and accurately described them, something later writers seldom did. Even when he returned to Spain, he remained a defender of the natives and railed at the Spanish enslavement of the Indians.

Cabeza de Vaca is nearly forgotten in the United States but remains famous in Spain. *Florida Archives.*

His journey inspired later expeditions led by Hernando de Soto and Francisco Coronado. As a reward, the Spanish Crown named him head of the government in Argentina, but his leadership was criticized and he returned to Spain, where he died penniless.

ANONYMOUS

The first poem about North America was placed in the Bodleian Library at Oxford University in 1564, and the author is unknown.

The poem is titled, "The preme Rose in the grene forest." The section dealing with Florida is known as "Have You Not Hard of Floryda." It is unclear whether this was one poem or two poems cobbled together. Also unknown is when the stanzas were written, whether others were added and if some may have been lost. It is thought that stanzas four and five may be from a poem written later and inserted into this one.

It is the first poetic commentary on Florida and the first recorded poem written about North America. The poem is written in English, and it is doubtful that it could have been written by a member of either the Spanish or French expeditions of the sixteenth century.

The Spanish expeditions at one point claimed lands as far north as president-day Virginia, and it is possible an English expedition was referring to those lands. Florida did not get its name until 1513, when Ponce de Leon sailed along the coast.

And as I walked toward s poles [St. Pauls]
I met a frend of myne,
Who toke [me] *by the hand and sayde,*
"Com drynk a pynt of wyne,
Wher you shall here [hear]
Such news, I fere,
As you abrode wyll compell.
with hy!

Have you not hard of floryda,
A coontre far bewest,
Where savage pepell planted are
By nature and by hest,
Who in the mold
Fynd glysterynge gold
and yt for tryfels sell?
with hy!

Ye all alonge the watere side,
Where yt doth eb and flowe,
Are turkeyse founde and where also
Do perles in oysteres growe,
And on the land
Do cedars stand
Whose bewty do[th] *excel.*
with hy!
trysky, trym, go trysky, wun not a wallet do well?

The prymerose in the greene forest,
The vyolets the grow gaye,
The Dubbell Dayses with the rest
So merryly deks the waye
To moove my Sprytes
Through fond delyghts
Lyke pretty wons as the be.
with hy!

The sweete record, the nytyngale,
The leveret and the thrushe,

Which whyps & skyps & wages there tales
From every bank to busshe
And chyrpyngly
Do pas the day
Like prety wond as the be.

Have over the water to floryda,
Farewell, gay lundon, nowe,
Throw long deles by land and sese,
I am brawght, I cannot tell howe,
To plymwoorthe towne
In a thredbare goowne
and mony never Dele
with hy!
wunnot a wallet do well?

When Aprell sylver showers so sweet
Can make may flowers to sprynge
And every pretty byrd prepars
Her wystlyng throte to synge,
The nyghtyngale
In every Dale
They doth ther duty well.
with hy!

NICOLAS LE CHALLEUX

While a vast library of writings by Spanish writers survives, the French presence in Florida was brief and bloody. The Spanish came to Florida first but expressed little interest in colonizing an area with no mineral wealth. That changed with the arrival of the French. The Spanish Catholics would not allow French Protestants to convert the Native Americans to Protestantism, and the Spanish wanted a site on Florida's east coast to protect their gold-laden ships sailing for Spain.

The two sides were destined to clash after the French built Fort Caroline near present-day Jacksonville.

The French sailed for St. Augustine to confront the Spanish, but their ship was caught in a storm and the French soldiers washed ashore, where the waiting Spanish put them to death.

Nicolas Le Challeux came to Florida with the French expedition and was one of the few survivors. He escaped and returned to France, where he wrote a poem that summarized his time in Florida:

> *Whoever wishes to go to Florida,*
> *Let him go where I have been.*
> *And return dry and arid,*
> *And worn out by rot.*
> *For the only good I have brought back—*
> *A single silvery stick in my hand.*
> *But I am safe, not defeated:*
> *It's time to eat; I die of hunger.*

His primary contribution was a book about the French struggles in Florida, which includes his vivid description of the slaughter by the Spanish. The book, *Nicolas Le Challeux's Narrative of Captain Jean Ribault's Last Voyage in 1565, Undertaken at the King's Command, to an Island in the Indies Commonly Called Florida*, is the first history of Florida. The book was published in France in 1566 shortly after Challeux returned.

ALONSO GREGORIO DE ESCOBEDO

De Vaca was not the only friend the Indians found among the early Spanish. Friar Alonso Gregorio de Escobedo arrived in St. Augustine in 1587 and immediately began writing about what he saw. His poem contains 21,000 lines filling 449 pages. The work has never been published and has been read by only a few in the Biblioteca Nacional in Madrid. He writes in a stream of consciousness and jumps from one topic to another, making it almost impossible to understand.

One minute he is writing about Indian fishing and the next composing one of his sermons, followed by an account of his day in Florida. It is unfortunate his writings have not received more attention, since he does provide an honest look at life in Florida and, like De Vaca, is sympathetic to the Indians.

JUAN DE CASTELLANOS

Juan de Castellanos was born in 1522, one year after Juan Ponce de Leon died, yet it is Castellanos who became the source for myths about Ponce and the Fountain of Youth. Castellanos arrived in Puerto Rico in the 1540s and began writing poetry—a total of 113,000 lines in four volumes.

Castellanos devotes most of his poem to Ponce discovering Florida, but it was the section on the Fountain of Youth that captivated the world. Bimini is a small island off the southeast coast of Florida, although it shows up often in Spanish literature and could mean Florida itself or a nearby island.

The myth of the Fountain of Youth began nearly 2,500 years ago, beginning with Herodotus, who said it was in Somalia. Later it was said to be in Asia, and by the twelfth century it was said to have been found by the Crusaders.

Parts of Castellanos's work were published in 1589, but it was another 250 years before they were all published. He wrote a poem linking Ponce to the fountain:

> *Amongst the most ancient of their people,*
> *There were many Indians who said that on Bimini, a powerful island*
> *And center for many different nations, there exists a fountain with great virtues*
> *From which older men became young again*
> *And where elderly women walked away*
> *With wrinkles smoothed over and hair not grey.*

Although the poem did not claim Ponce found a Fountain of Youth, it linked him forever with the fountain. Over the past four centuries, there have been various claims about the location in Florida. An attraction in St. Augustine claims to be the real Fountain of Youth, but dozens of other sites have made similar claims.

JONATHAN DICKINSON

Jonathan Dickinson had no intention of coming to Florida in 1696 when he and his family sailed from Jamaica bound for Philadelphia. Dickinson, his wife, their infant son and ten slaves set off on the *Reformation* as part of a convoy. Their ship became separated from the rest, and after three weeks, a violent storm struck and their ship ran aground at what is now Hobe Sound.

Dickinson's book has remained in print for more than three hundred years. *Yale University Press.*

They were confronted by the Jaega Indians, who stole their provisions and took them prisoner. At Jupiter Inlet, the Indians burned their ship, sparing only a lifeboat, then released the party except for a young slave.

They split into two groups; the children and sick were put into the lifeboat and rowed up the coast while the rest walked along the shore. A second tribe, the Ais Indians, took them next and continued their journey. At Vero Beach, they were surprised to find a friendly welcome, and the Indians allowed them to send one member of the party to St. Augustine to seek help.

On November 2, Spanish soldiers arrived, but it was not quite the salvation they sought. The journey to St. Augustine was difficult, and five died of exposure and hunger. The Spanish gave them boats for the journey to Charles Town, South Carolina, and they finally reached Philadelphia seven months after they left Port Royal.

Dickinson wrote about his ordeal in what became known as *Jonathan Dickinson's Journal*, which is a short version of one of the longest titles in literature:

> *God's Protecting Providence Man's Surest Help and Defence in the Times of the Greatest Difficulty and Most Imminent Danger Evidenced in the Remarkable Deliverance of Robert Barrow, With Divers Other Persons, from the Devouring Waves of the Sea, amongst which They Suffered Shipwreck. And also, From the Cruel Devouring Jaws of the Inhumane Canibals* [sic] *of Florida. Faithfully Related by One of the Persons Concerned Therein, Jonathan Dickinson.*

When he reached Philadelphia, seven months after sailing from Jamaica, he published his story in a thin volume. It quickly became a huge success, giving many their first detailed look at Florida and the Indian tribes. The *Cambridge History of English and American Literature* called it "in many respects the best of all the captivity tracts."

It was not only a rousing adventure story, but the Quakers also saw it as an inspirational story because Dickinson did not use force, despite the dangers.

Earlier works were written in Spanish and French, and for many in England, this was their first look at Florida. The tract was reprinted in English sixteen times and went through multiple printings in Dutch and German. Dickinson became one of Philadelphia's leading citizens, serving two terms as mayor and accumulating vast wealth.

FLORIDA TRAVELERS

WILLIAM BARTRAM

When Jules Verne sat down to write *From the Earth to the Moon*, he wanted to learn about Florida, the site he selected for the launch of the rocket to the moon. One of the books he read was *Travels*, the classic work by naturalist William Bartram.

Bartram failed at a lengthy list of pursuits, including artist, surveyor, merchant and farmer. He created a plantation near present-day Jacksonville in 1766 and worked the land for several years before giving up and returning to his father's Philadelphia home.

In 1772, Dr. John Fothergill hired Bartram to collect natural history specimens for £150 a year. Fothergill was looking for plants that would grow in England, although why Fothergill thought that Florida plants would withstand the bitter English winter is a mystery.

From 1773 to 1777, Bartram traveled through the American Southeast, recording details of the plants, people and animals he encountered.

After working in Georgia, he moved to Florida in 1774, landing first at Amelia Island and inspecting the indigo crops. On the Florida mainland, he found the orange trees in bloom as he traveled up the St. Johns River to Palatka, then a major port and a resort for those seeking relief from consumption.

A band of Seminoles named him Puc-puggee, the Flower Hunter. His writings showed remarkable sympathy and friendship for the Indians, something rare in English writing.

William Bartram's book documenting his travels with a bestseller in the American colonies and in Europe. *Library of Congress.*

His book *Travels Through North and South Carolina, Georgia, East and West Florida, etc.*, became a bestseller in the American colonies, but its greatest popularity was in Europe, where it was translated into several languages.

Bartram's problem was that he was too successful. Because he found previously unknown plants and animals, there was widespread speculation that he was writing fiction, and many doubted his findings.

The British poets William Wadsworth and Samuel Taylor Coleridge and the French writer François-René Chateaubriand used Bartram's writings as inspiration for their work. Coleridge read *Travels* about eight years after it was published, and the work influenced his poems written in 1797 and 1798. Coleridge wrote, "It is a work of high merit everyway." Readers can see Bartram's influence in Coleridge's *The Rime of the Ancient Mariner* and *Kubla Khan*. In *Kubla Khan*, Coleridge writes about an untamed place, inspired by Bartram's description of Florida. Wordsworth also relied on Bartram for his works, including *The Prelude* and *A Guide Through the Lake District*.

After reading Bartram's work, Chateaubriand was inspired to come to Florida and write his novel *Atala*. Although he claims to have relied on his own experiences, it is clear he borrowed much from Bartram's work.

JOHN MUIR

John Muir might have spent his entire life making wagon wheels if an accident had not damaged his eyes. Doctors told him to remain in a darkened room for six weeks as the only treatment available. The time in the darkness led him to reevaluate his life. "God has to nearly kill us sometimes to teach us lessons."

In 1867, he quit his job and spent the rest of his life studying nature. He decided to walk the thousand miles from Indiana to Florida, passing through Kentucky, Tennessee and Georgia on his way. "Today, at last, I reached Florida," he wrote in his diary.

He stopped in Fernandina Beach, today a charming resort town, but then one of the state's largest cities, with a bustling seaport.

Three days later, he reached Gainesville, following the tracks of the state's railroad from Fernandina to Cedar Key on the Gulf of Mexico, although much of the track was damaged during the Civil War.

> *I was meeting so many strange plants that I was much excited, making many stops to get specimens. But I could not force my way through the swampy forest, although so tempting and full of promise. Regardless of water snakes or insects, I endeavored repeatedly to force a way through the tough vine-tangles, but seldom succeeded in getting farther than a few hundred yards.*

Cedar Key is a pleasant coastal community today, but it was once an industrial center, famous throughout the world for its cedar trees used in the manufacture of pencils. The Eberhard Faber Company built the first mill, followed by the Eagle Pencil Company.

At the same, lumber from the area was being used to repair the railroad, creating a boom for the town.

The mechanical skills Muir learned making wagon wheels came in handy in Cedar Key. He was hired to fix machinery at a local sawmill, and his skills proved invaluable. In Cedar Key, he came down with malaria, a not uncommon occurrence in a state where mosquitoes were everywhere. He recovered at the home of the sawmill manager while working on his book, *A Thousand-Mile Walk to the Gulf.* While recovering, he spent hours lying in the woods staring at the trees and plants. "I crept away to the edge of the wood, and sat day after day beneath a moss-draped live-oak."

He scrapped plans to continue his walk to South America and took a schooner to Cuba. From Cuba, he sailed to New York, then traveled to California, where he made his reputation as a naturalist.

In 1898, he returned to Florida and Cedar Key. He visited the woman who had nursed him when he had malaria, telling her, "I promised to come back and visit you in about twenty-five years, and though a little late I've come."

JOHN JAMES AUDUBON

John James Audubon was working as a storekeeper in Kentucky, struggling to survive, when he gave up the store to become a portrait painter. His fortunes did not improve much as he went from town to town seeking clients on the frontier who wanted a portrait painted.

John Audubon made several trips to Florida to capture birds and write short stories. *Library of Congress.*

As he traveled, he painted the birds he saw and received encouragement for a massive undertaking, painting the birds of North America.

He arrived in Florida in 1831, but his timing was terrible—the Seminole War was underway, making travel outside of St. Augustine dangerous. He found lodgings at a local tavern, where he found his fellow boarders disagreeable. He asked his wife to send him more socks, finding, "the salt marshes through which I am forced to wade every day are the ruin of everything."

His days became routine: "We get into a boat, and after an hour of hard rowing, we find ourselves in the middle of the most extensive marshes as far as the eye can reach. The boat is anchored, and we go wading through mud and water, amid myriads of sandflies and mosquitoes, shooting here and there a bird." He complained that St. Augustine residents were too lazy to help him in his work.

He lasted in Florida only a few months, worrying that his dog, Plato, would be devoured by the alligators. He retreated to Charleston but heard about a variety of birds in Key West and set sail. In Key West, he found a species he had only heard about. "Seldom have I experienced greater pleasures than when on the Florida Keys, under a burning sun, after pushing my bark for miles over a soapy flat." He found the nearly extinct white-crowned pigeon and the great white heron.

However, he had mixed feelings about the Keys. He was afraid of yellow fever and refused to spend nights on the island. Instead, he worked during the day on the island, then slept on board a ship anchored offshore.

Audubon is remembered for his paintings of birds, but he also wrote short stories based on tales he heard during his travels. In the Keys, he heard the story about a dying pirate who was found in a boat stained with blood with two dead men inside. The man urged the pirate to confess his sins and clear his conscience, "'Friend,' said he, 'for friend you seems to be, I have never studied the ways of Him of whom you talk. I am an outlaw, perhaps you will say a wretch—I have been for many years a pirate."

In addition to "Death of a Pirate," he wrote "The Wreckers of Florida," "Long Calm at Sea" and "Florida Keys."

Audubon's findings were so amazing that many people thought they did not exist. *Library of Congress.*

It is called the Audubon House because John Audubon once painted a bird in a tree on the property. The house was built after Audubon visited the island. *Florida Archives.*

The problem with Audubon's stories is that it is impossible to know whether they are fiction or nonfiction. Perhaps they do contain some facts; perhaps they are just old sea tales. The Second Seminole War forced him to cancel plans to return to the Florida peninsula, although he did make it to Pensacola.

THEY NEVER SAW FLORIDA

SAMUEL TAYLOR COLERIDGE

As soon as Ponce de Leon spotted Florida in 1513, the myths began. Mountains were running down the center of the state, the manatees were mermaids and rivers flowed through the state, connecting the Atlantic with the Gulf of Mexico. Between 1773 and 1776, William Bartram came through the South capturing what he saw in his book *Travels Through North & South Carolina, Georgia, East & West Florida, etc*. The book was published in 1791, and soon an edition appeared in England.

The book caused a sensation in England and was read by writers including Wordsworth and Coleridge. Wordsworth used Florida in one of his poems, *Ruth*, drawing from Bartram and using Florida as an exotic place of mystery.

> *He spake of plants divine and strange*
> *That every hour their blossoms change,*
> *Ten thousand lovely hues!*
> *With budding, fading, faded flowers.*

Coleridge was one of the founders of the Romantic Movement and made extensive notes from Bartram in his journals. He used the notes in writing his two most famous poems, *Kubla Khan* and *The Rime of the Ancient Mariner*. As he fell into an opium-induced sleep he was reading Bartram, and when he awoke he wrote *Kubla Khan*.

Samuel Coleridge is believed to have based his poem *Kubla Khan* on a Florida spring near Ocala.

> *In Xanadu did Kubla Khan*
> *A Stately pleasure-dome decry*
> *Where Alph, the sacred river, ran*
> *Through caverns measureless to man*
>   *Down to a sunless sea,*
> *So twice five miles of fertile ground*
> *With walls and towers were girdled round;*
> *And there were gardens bright with sinuous rills,*
> *Where blossomed many an incense-bearing tree;*
> *And here were forests ancient as the hills,*
> *Enfolding sunny spots of greenery.*

Manatee Springs near Gainesville or Salt Springs in the Ocala National Forest are believed to be the springs he wrote about, and Salt Springs Run is the river.

OLIVER WENDELL HOLMES

Oliver Wendell Holmes was one of the great minds of the nineteenth century. He was a physician, poet and author and spent his adult life teaching medicine at Harvard University.

In his sixties, he turned to thoughts of growing old and to the myth of a Fountain of Youth. Holmes read his poem to his classmates forty-four years after graduating from Harvard. Like him, they were approaching seventy years of age and reflecting on their youth:

> *The fount the Spaniard sought in vain*
> *Through all the land of flowers*
> *Leaps glittering from the sandy plain*
> *Our classic grove embowers;*
> *Here youth, unchanging, blooms and smiles,*
> *Here dwells eternal spring,*
> *And warm from Hope's elysian isles*
> *The winds their perfume bring...*

JULES VERNE

Jules Verne was about one hundred years and one hundred miles off, but his fantasy of spacecraft leaving Florida for the moon became a reality. Verne created the science fiction writing genre and brought worldwide attention to the little-known state and an almost unknown town, Tampa.

Verne studied law but was drawn to writing. While he struggled to make a living at first, by his mid-thirties, he had produced a string of bestsellers that are still in print 150 years later: *Journey to the Center of the Earth*, *Twenty Thousand Leagues Under the Sea* and *Around the World in Eighty Days*.

From the Earth to the Moon remains the most amazing because of the research Verne did.

For his research, Verne consulted the available books about Florida and shared his findings with his readers. In *From the Earth to the Moon*, Verne's missile launch is underwritten by a Baltimore gun club, which has to choose between Texas and Florida as the launch site. A century later, Texas and Florida would compete for control of the space program.

Verne liberally borrowed from the descriptions in these texts. While he gets many things right, some things are very wrong. He places Tampa at 1,800 feet above sea level, about 1,750 feet above its true height. When the real launch site was selected, it was on the Florida's east coast. And he had buffalo roaming the state.

The book includes an attack by the Seminole Indians against the moon travelers.

Not only was Florida the site of the real moon launch in 1969, but both Verne and NASA decided on a three-member crew for the journey. Verne called the device used to launch the spacecraft the *Columbiad*, and the Apollo 11 command module was named *Columbia*.

Both Verne's craft and NASA's returned by splashing down in the Pacific and were fished out by a U.S. Navy ship. As the astronauts of Apollo 11—the first to land on the moon—sped homeward on July 23, 1969, Mission Commander Neil Armstrong said,

> *A hundred years ago, Jules Verne wrote a book about a voyage to the Moon. His spaceship* Columbia *[sic] took off from Florida and landed in the Pacific Ocean after completing a trip to the Moon. It seems appropriate to us to share with you some of the reflections of the crew as the modern-day* Columbia *completes its rendezvous with the planet Earth and the same Pacific Ocean tomorrow.*

Verne's 1867 trip to the United States, two years after the book's publication, did not include Florida.

WALT WHITMAN

On the wall of Walt Whitman's Camden, New Jersey study was a drawing of the great Florida Indian Chief Osceola. When he was given the drawing, supposedly by the artist George Catlin, it was frayed, and Whitman spent hours putting it together. With the portrait of the chief hanging in his study, Whitman wrote a tribute to the chief in 1890.

Whitman said, "When I was nearly grown to manhood in Brooklyn, New York (middle of 1838), I met one of the return'd U.S. Marines from Fort Moultrie, S.C., and had long talks with him—learn'd the occurrence below described—death of Osceola."

Osceola led attacks against American soldiers in Florida, striking fear among the settlers who lived on the frontier. The U.S. Army offered Osceola a truce to negotiate terms. When he agreed to negotiate, he was captured by soldiers and imprisoned. He died in captivity, and his head was cut off by the attending physician and ended up in a museum.

The deceit used to capture Osceola and his fate turned him from a villain into a sympathetic figure. As Whitman wrote, Osceola was "basely betrayed, imprisoned, and literally done to death."

When his hour for death had come,
He slowly rais'd himself from the bed on the floor,
Drew on his war-dress, shirt, leggings, and girdled the belt around his waist,
Call'd for vermilion paint (his looking glass was held before him,)
Painted half his face and neck, his wrists, and back-hands.
Put the scalp-knife carefully in his belt—then lying down, resting a moment,
Rose again, half sitting, smiled, gave in silence his extended hand to each
    and all,
Sank faintly low to the floor (tightly grasping the tomahawk handle,)
Fix'd his look on wife and little children—the last:
(And here a line in memory of his name and death.)

Whitman's most popular Florida poem was written during a blizzard gripping the Northeast:

A lesser proof than old Voltaire's, yet greater, *
Proof of this present time, and thee, thy broad expanse, America,
To my plain Northern hut, in outside clouds and snow,
Brought safely for a thousand miles o'er land and tide,
Some three days since on their own soil live sprouting,
Now here their sweetness through my room unfolding,
A bunch of orange buds by mail from Florida.

*Voltaire wrote that great ships and the opera were proof of civilization.

In the frigid North, the poem struck just the right note and was reprinted in newspapers throughout the frozen states.

OLIVER GOLDSMITH

Oliver Goldsmith never saw Florida, but one of his best-known poems deals with the place.

Britain acquired Florida from Spain in 1763 at the end of the French and Indian War. England was anxious to convert its new colony from Spanish rule to British, and that would require an influx of new citizens. There was little in Florida to attract new residents; it was a raw frontier with threatening Indians, swamps and yellow fever.

To help attract residents, the British government began giving away land in Florida—in all, more than three million acres. It drew thousands of people, and Goldsmith noticed the exodus from England.

Goldsmith was born in 1830, and smallpox left him deformed and the victim of bullies. He failed at medical and law schools and turned to writing and found success in 1766 with *The Vicar of Wakefield.*

"The Deserted Village" observes the changes in what Goldsmith calls "Sweet Auburn," which is probably his hometown. He laments the exodus of the citizens while denigrating America.

To Goldsmith, America is a land of savage men and hideous animals. He thought Florida was dreary and warned of the blazing sun and intolerable days. He could not imagine the villagers giving up their lovely village for a land of snakes and tigers. Goldsmith begins by describing the wonders of Sweet Auburn, then turns to the horrors of Florida:

> *The various terrors of that horrid shore;*
> *Those blazing suns that dart a downward ray,*
> *And fiercely shed intolerable day;*
> *Those matted woods where birds forget to sing,*
> *But silent bats in drowsy clusters cling;*
> *Those poisonous fields with rank luxuriance crowned,*
> *Where the dark scorpion gathers death around;*
> *Where at each step the stranger fears to wake*
> *The rattling terrors of the vengeful snake;*
> *Where crouching tigers wait their hapless prey,*
> *And savage men, more murderous still than they;*
> *While oft in whirls the mad tornado flies,*
> *Mingling the ravaged landscape with the skies,*
> *Far different these from every former scene,*
> *The cooling brook, the grassy vested green…*

British rule ended in 1783 with the end of the American Revolution—this time Britain was on the losing side—and Spain regained control. The offers of land in Florida ended.

THE JOURNALISTS

FREDERICK REMINGTON

By the 1890s, Frederick Remington was running out of frontier. The census of 1890 determined that the West was settled, leaving southwest Florida as the final frontier. With the end of the western frontier came the end of the things Remington cherished and had captured so brilliantly in his words, drawings and statues.

After 1894, Remington made no western excursions, but his search for the frontier, cowboys and adventure was not over. In 1895, *Harper's Weekly* sent Remington to southwest Florida to capture this last frontier in drawings and words. The frontier and the cowboys were far different from the West he loved.

Southwest Florida was lightly populated and every bit as wild as the West. It remained a frontier almost until World War II. In 1937, a cattleman drove a herd of cattle 160 miles without encountering any fences or people.

Remington went to Punta Gorda and Arcadia and invited his close friend Owen Wister, the author of the western classic *The Virginian*, to join him. He promised Wister, "Bear, tarpon, red snapper, ducks, birds of paradise" if he came. And he told him there would be "curious cowboys who shoot up the railroad trains."

Remington, whose work had glorified the western cowboys, was not impressed with the Florida version. When he first saw them, he wrote:

Frederick Remington came to Florida in search of cowboys but left disappointed. *Author's collection.*

"Two very emaciated Texas ponies pattered down the street; bearing wild-looking individuals…[with] hanging hair and drooping hats and generally bedraggled appearance." The two cowboys tied up their horses, entered a saloon and were drunk within fifteen minutes. He found the Florida cowboys slovenly, drunken, dishonest and unromantic—they did not even wear cowboy boots, choosing the shoes of a farmer.

He did find many things he had found in the West: cattle stealing, gunfire and a propensity by law enforcement to look the other way. When a cowboy was shot while trying to rebrand a stolen steer, the coroner's jury decided he had died when he fell on the animal's horns.

It wasn't just the cowboys who disappointed Remington; he even found fault with the cows. Cattle were first brought over by the Spanish beginning in the 1500s. The Florida cows were scrawny when compared with the magnificent animals that roamed the West.

Despite his views, he was back a year later to cover the growing crisis in Cuba. He and veteran reporter Richard Harding Davis stopped in Key West en route to Cuba—Davis would provide the words and Remington the drawings. They were on assignment for William Randolph Hearst's *New York Journal*, which was leading the call for war with Spain.

They were stuck in Key West as Spain erected a blockade around its possession. They tried to use Hearst's powerboat to outrun the blockade but turned back after running into foul weather.

After several weeks, they were able to book passage on a commercial ship. It could not have been soon enough for Remington, who hated Key

One of Remington's drawings shows cowboys driving off rustlers. *Author's collection.*

West. He said the "sun makes men sweat and wish to God they were somewhere else."

He may have hated Key West, but he returned as the war grew closer, joining scores of other journalists waiting for American entry into the war.

When he made it to Cuba, there was little to write about.

Hearst's constant drumbeat for war, combined with the explosion of the USS *Maine*, led to war and sent Remington to Tampa, where he joined thousands of troops preparing to embark to Cuba. He stayed at the Tampa Bay Hotel, the finest in town and home to dozens of reporters, generals and those seeking to do business with the army.

As with Key West, he was not impressed with Tampa, saying it was "chiefly composed of derelict houses drifting on an ocean of sand." His drawings captured the military buildup in Tampa, displaying a complete range—officers, animals, and enlisted men.

Finally, he sailed for Cuba aboard the headquarters ship. He came down with yellow fever and was repulsed by the dead bodies. "From now on I mean to paint fruits and flowers," he wrote.

STEPHEN CRANE

By 1896, Jacksonville had become the gateway to Florida, drawing visitors from the North who came for the warm weather and to board ships to Cuba and the Caribbean.

In 1896, the city became the center for gunrunning to revolutionary Cuba. People were seeking to get rich by selling guns, shipowners were looking for a cargo to smuggle, journalists were reporting for a story and spies operated on both sides of the revolution.

Among the reporters was Stephen Crane, who made his fame with the Civil War book *The Red Badge of Courage*. He was covering the war and searching Jacksonville for a ship to take him to Cuba.

Much of Crane's success was due to Irving Bacheller, who created the first newspaper syndicate. He acquired rights to books, broke them into parts and sold them to newspapers, which promoted them to increase circulation. In addition to Crane, he represented Arthur Conan Doyle and Rudyard Kipling. Bacheller dispatched Crane to Jacksonville to write articles for his newspaper syndicate.

Crane used the alias Samuel Carleton, allowing him to move about without being a celebrity. He assumed one of the many ships in the harbor would take him to Cuba, but while the captains were prepared to run guns, they wanted no passengers who might cause problems.

He checked in at the St. James Hotel, the finest in town, and soon became a fixture at Huau's cigar store on Main Street, which was the center of activity for all sides in the revolution. It was a strange mix; Jose Marti, the leader of the revolution, could be seen there along with Spanish agents, Pinkerton detectives, gunrunners and camp followers. The Spanish spies were so obvious that the *Daily Florida Citizen* reported that Carleton (Crane) and two other men were "being closely watched by Spanish spies." The Spanish believed Crane was a former soldier working with the rebels.

As the days dragged on, Crane began frequenting the bars and brothels, where business was booming. It was in one of the brothels that he met Cora Taylor, a madam who ran a house called the Court.

The relationship between Cora and Crane turned into more than a business arrangement. Her interest in Crane increased once she learned he was a famous writer.

On the final day of 1896, he was able to book passage on the *Commodore*, which was packed with forty bundles of rifles and more than 200,000 shells.

Stephen Crane met his future wife while attempting to cover the revolution in Cuba.
Florida Archives.

The ship was just two miles offshore when things began to go badly. The ship became stuck on a sandbar and needed help to escape.

Things became worse. The captain became seasick and was of little use; then the ship began taking on water. The pumps failed, and the passengers and crew formed a human bucket brigade to keep the rising water from swamping the boat.

The ship was thirteen miles off the coast of Florida when it began to sink. Amid the confusion, three lifeboats were launched, but Crane, the captain and a few others were left to seek salvation in a dinghy.

Crane began 1897 in a small dinghy.

One of the lifeboats reached the shore the following morning, and a second came two hours later. When the third boat arrived, it was empty.

Crane's dinghy finally washed ashore near Daytona Beach, although one of the passengers drowned as they approached the shore. When word reached Jacksonville, the accounts were confusing.

Four days later, he was back in Jacksonville and wearing the same clothes as he walked into the lobby of the hotel to a cheering crowd. His rescue was front-page news throughout the country, including the *New York Times.*

He initially wrote a one-thousand-word story about his ordeal and then began work on a second longer version, which became "The Open Boat." He dropped his plans to go to Cuba and on the train ride to New York wrote the longer version for *Scribner's Magazine.*

Cora was legally married to a British military officer but became Crane's common-law wife. He died in 1900, and Cora eventually returned to her life as a successful bordello owner in Jacksonville.

H.L. MENCKEN

On May 3, 1901, workers at the Cleveland Fiber Factory in downtown Jacksonville went to lunch. Within minutes, a fire started in a pile of Spanish moss. The wind carried the sparks, and in eight hours the fire burned 146 city blocks, destroying nearly 2,368 buildings. It was the largest urban fire in the southeastern United States.

Newspaper reporters descended on the city from all over the country to record the damage and the misery. The *Baltimore Morning Herald* sent twenty-three-year-old H.L. Mencken to cover the story, his first out-of-town assignment after just two years as a full-time reporter.

Many of the newspaper reporters were there not so much to report on the fire and its aftermath but to cover efforts by their hometowns to help the fire victims. Often the drive to help Jacksonville was organized by newspapers, so the reporters were there to promote their newspapers.

Mencken captured the mood in his memoirs:

> *But what so powerfully reinformed my growing suspicion of service was not this scene of desolation, but the imbecility of the public effort to aid to ostensible victims. In every American community of Christian pretensions, North, East, South and West, busy bodies began to collect money and goods for their succor the moment the first bulletins came in, and by the time I reached what was left of the Jacksonville railroad station the first relief shipments were on their way.*

The Jacksonville fire destroyed much of the city and brought scores of journalists to the town to document the damage, including H.L. Mencken. *Florida Archives.*

He was on his way to becoming one of the nation's leading journalists, covering everything from the Scopes Monkey Trial to World War II.

Mencken spent only a few days in Jacksonville, and it was half a century before he returned. Relaxing in St. Petersburg, he said he was having a good time until a local reporter printed a story that he was in town and he was besieged by people who wanted to meet the legendary journalist.

RING LARDNER

Ring Lardner was already one of the nation's best-known writers when he first came to Florida in 1926. Florida was at the height of the land boom, and Lardner was at the height of his career. Lardner once wrote that he had three goals: to see lots of baseball games, write for a magazine and produce a successful play. He accomplished all three.

He started as a sportswriter in Indiana and then moved to bigger newspapers in Chicago, Boston and St. Louis before returning to Chicago and the *Chicago Tribune*, where his syndicated column appeared in 135 newspapers. He drew the attention of the *Saturday Evening Post*, then the nation's leading magazine.

Spring training brought Lardner to Florida, and he came up with an idea for a movie set in Florida. It involves a baseball team caught up in the state's land boom and was one of the last silent movies ever filmed. In the movie, *The New Klondike*, the team pitcher talks his teammates into investing in Florida real estate, which turns out to be swampland.

He set two of his stories in Florida and included his own experiences. "Gullible's Travels," written in 1916, tells of a midwestern couple who visit Palm Beach. The couple believes the rate at the Royal Poinciana of seventeen dollars is within their reach but find out that the initial charge is just the beginning of the costs. The dining room is so large it is a long-distance call from one end to the other:

> *I promised the wife that if anybody ast me what kind of a time did I have at Palm Beach I'd say I had a swell time. And if they ast me who did we meet I'd tell 'em everybody that was worth meetin'. And if they ast me didn't the trip cost a lot I'd say Yes; but it was worth the money. I promised her I wouldn't spill none o' the real details. But if you can't break a promise you made to your own wife what kind of a promise can you break? Answer me that, Edgar.*

In "The Golden Honeymoon," Lardner also has fun with the Florida vacation with a couple celebrating their fiftieth anniversary with a trip to St. Petersburg. Just as Lardner was achieving his greatest success, his health declined. He suffered from heart problems and learned he had tuberculosis. In 1933, he suffered a heart attack and died at forty-eight.

DAMON RUNYON

As Damon Runyon lay dying alone in his New York hotel room, he was thinking about Florida. He captured Miami and its residents with his writing, but now he was thinking about the beautiful house he had built on Hibiscus Island off Miami for his wife, Patrice, and what would become of it when he died.

Runyon was a newspaperman and short story writer who populated his stories with characters real and imagined and caught the attention of the nation. He began his career in 1900 in Denver and then moved to New York in 1910, where he covered sports for the *New York American*. It was Runyon who nicknamed boxer James J. Braddock "Cinderella Man."

In Texas one year to cover baseball's spring training, he met the Mexican bandit and revolutionary leader Pancho Villa and later joined troops seeking to find Villa in Mexico.

In Mexico, he met Patrice Amati del Grande and financed her education. At the time, Runyon was married to Ellen Runyon, whose drinking became worse and worse during their twenty-eight-year marriage. When she died in 1932, he turned his attention to the young girl he had met in Mexico. Patrice moved to New York, where Runyon promised to find her a job. Even though she was twenty-six years younger than Runyon, they married the same year his wife died.

Runyon began visiting Miami in the 1920s, when the town was wide open, with land schemes, gangsters, illegal liquor and the horseracing Runyon loved. He created his own fractured English: head became *noggin*, a knife was a *shiv*, a grenade became a *pineapple* and a gun was a *roscoe* or *equalizer*.

His friends in Miami included gangster Al Capone, who purchased a mansion on Palm Island in 1928. The two were seen together frequently, and in 1929, Runyon served as a party planner and public relations man for Capone. A fight between Jack Sharkey and Young Stribling became the sporting event of the year, drawing forty thousand fans and more than four hundred journalists.

Damon Runyon left his Miami mansion to his former wife. *Florida Archives.*

Capone wanted to entertain the reporters and celebrities and turned to Runyon to help arrange it. On the night of the party, the journalists were searched for guns. One of the journalists stole a diamond ring belonging to Mrs. Capone.

Runyon was a regular at the Miami race tracks, Hialeah and Tropical, where he put two dollars on each horse, then claimed he had picked the winner. His system left him constantly in debt, with staggering losses. Parts of a short story he wrote, "Pick the Winner," were used in his Broadway play *Guys and Dolls*. It was Runyon who wrote the classic line, "The race is not always to the swift, nor the battle to the strong, but that's how the smart money bets."

He also wrote the classic line "sand in our shoes." He was supposed to travel to California to work on a movie for Paramount Studios, but he begged off, saying he wanted to remain in Miami because he had sand in his shoes.

He built a magnificent home for his new wife on Hibiscus Island, one of several islands between Miami and Miami Beach and close to the island where Capone lived. Runyon became known as the "Hermit of Hibiscus Island."

His health began to decline, and in 1944 his voice box was removed—the consequence of heavy smoking.

To recuperate, he moved to a New York hotel room, leaving his wife behind in the Miami mansion. There, she met a younger man and soon began an affair. Two years later, she divorced Runyon, who still loved her. He rewrote his will but still left her a portion of his estate. She received the Miami house and an interest in his writings, which turned out to be substantial—she received part royalties from the play and movie *Guys and Dolls*.

When Runyon died, the *Miami Herald* wrote, "Miami loved Runyon and the famous newspaper reporter, columnist, and fiction writer reciprocated in the fullest."

Several of his stories, including "Palm Beach Santa Claus" and two others, were published in *Runyon a la Carte* three years after his death. "Palm Beach Santa Claus" appeared in *Collier's* magazine in 1938.

"Palm Beach Santa Claus" features a down-on-his-luck Runyon character who ends up being hired to be a Santa Claus for a wealthy Palm Beach matron.

PAT FRANK

Pat Frank began as a young stringer at the *Jacksonville Journal* and went on to become a foreign correspondent in World War II and write a bestselling novel about a small Florida town following a nuclear attack.

He was known as much for his heavy drinking and debauchery as his writing. His drinking binges lasted for days.

Frank started as a teenaged Atlantic Beach correspondent for the *Journal*, being paid by how much he wrote. As his need for money increased, he drifted into fiction, stories all told at great length for a man being paid for each inch of type.

He was good enough to land a job at the *Washington Times-Herald*, where he became "the paper's crime and disaster expert, in attendance at every throat-slitting, husband poisoning, and 'I-killed-him-because-I-loved-him' episode on the Atlantic seaboard, plus kidnappings, floods, the World Series, and the opening days in Congress and at Pimlico," according to the *New York Times*, October 13, 1964.

During World War II, he worked for the Office of Strategic Services—the forerunner of the CIA—then returned to journalism reporting from Turkey, Austria, Germany and Italy, where he saw the body of Mussolini hanging in Milan. After the war, he returned to Atlantic Beach and turned to writing and politics—he traveled with John Kennedy during the 1960 presidential campaign.

He did much of his writing in Atlantic Beach, turning out eight books in all, in addition to magazine articles. His best-known article became the Rock Hudson movie *Man's Favorite Sport?*

Frank's first novel, *Mr. Adam*, was published in 1946 and sold two million copies. It is a satire about the single fertile man left on earth after a nuclear disaster. He had found his theme. In 1956, he published *Forbidden Area*, in which Russians land on a North Florida beach to bring the world close to nuclear war.

Frank followed that book with his most successful novel, *Alas, Babylon*, in 1959. While *Forbidden Area* took the world to the brink of nuclear war, *Alas, Babylon* brought the attack, with millions dead and those who were left facing "a thousand-year night." It became an episode on the *Playhouse 90* starring Dana Andrews, Rita Moreno and a young Burt Reynolds.

In the book, the end comes in Fort Repose, Florida, which is Mount Dora. Fort Repose is thrown into chaos as money becomes worthless, jail inmates escape and the surviving citizens realize that the world is in ruins and most of the government leadership is dead. The book remains a solid seller more than half a century after its publication

He wrote *Alas, Babylon* in Mount Dora while living with his last wife, Dodie, who managed to keep him sober and writing. Once they divorced, the heavy drinking resumed, and he became a full-fledged alcoholic.

Pat Frank's reward for helping the Kennedy campaign was a job in the civil defense department, where he wrote a book explaining how to survive a nuclear attack. He returned to Atlantic Beach in 1964 to die. Decades of drinking took their toll, and the cause of death was listed as inflammation of the pancreas. Frank was fifty-seven years old.

DAVE BARRY

Dave Barry never thought he would become the nation's top humor writer. He grew up in Armonk, New York, the son of a minister, and went to Pleasantville High School, then on to Haverford College near Philadelphia. He worked for the Episcopal Church for two years—instead of military service—and then joined the *Daily Local News*, a small newspaper outside Philadelphia. In 1975, he moved to the Associated Press in Philadelphia but found the job mind-numbing.

He might have spent his career grinding away at the Associated Press, but then one of those strange twists occurred. A friend offered him a job teaching writing to business executives. The course offered people a chance to write in simple English instead of the bureaucratic language that is so common in business communications.

Barry's presentations gave him a chance to try out his humor, and he found willing audiences. His wife suggested staying in journalism with a weekly column in his old newspaper. The column became a hit, and soon editors at other newspapers took notice. There were hundreds of newspaper columnists, many attempting to be funny. The *Washington Post* had Art Buchwald, and the *New York Times* had Russell Baker, but Barry's humor lacked any pretense—what other columnist would compare wine to bat urine?

In 1981, he gained national attention with a column on childbirth for the *Philadelphia Inquirer.* An editor at the *Miami Herald* saw the column, and two years later Barry joined the newspaper as a humor columnist. The *Herald*, one of the nation's top newspapers, was part of the Knight Ridder newspaper chain, and the company's syndicate gave him a national audience.

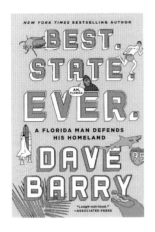

Dave Barry moved to Florida to work for the *Miami Herald* and found plenty to make fun of in Florida.

In the late 1980s, the *New York Times* published a lengthy, critical story about Miami—a popular subject for journalists looking for a story and warm weather. Barry responded with a hilarious send-up of life in New York City. "New York has more commissioners than Des Moines, Iowa, has residents," and cited the mythical "Commissioner for Bicycle Messengers Bearing Down on You at Warp Speed with Mohawk Haircuts and Pupils Smaller Than Purely Theoretical Particles."

That article, along with several others, including a moving piece about his mother, won him a Pulitzer Prize in 1989. His column appeared in five hundred newspapers, and his books made regular appearances on the bestseller list. Barry's life became a television series, *Dave's World*, which ran for four seasons on CBS.

He stopped writing his weekly column in 2005 while continuing to write books and contributing occasional columns. In all, he wrote more than two dozen books.

CARL HIAASEN

His grandfather—also named Carl—came from Norway, one of the millions of immigrants who flocked to the United States, settling in the Dakotas, a prime gathering place for Scandinavians. The government offered 160 acres to anyone who would work the land for five years.

Another land rush brought the family to Florida in the 1920s. The elder Carl settled in South Florida and opened a law office representing the land buyers and sellers who were changing the face of Florida. His son, Odel, joined him in the law firm, and in 1953, Odel's son, Carl, was born in Plantation. Although he was named after his grandfather, the two came to have far different views of land development in Florida.

The Plantation of his childhood featured open spaces and plenty of trees and brush. As Hiaasen grew up, he could see the open spaces giving way to developers.

He began writing in high school, producing a satirical newspaper called *More Trash*, and found he could make people laugh. He attended Emory

University for two years, then transferred to the University of Florida to major in journalism. He started at a small newspaper in Cocoa, then moved to the *Miami Herald*, the state's largest newspaper.

A friend at the *Herald*, William Montalbano, suggested they write a book, which led to three novels. The duo might have continued writing together, but Montalbano went to China as a foreign correspondent and Hiaasen began to write books on his own.

In 1986, he wrote *Tourist Season*, an instant hit, about a newspaper columnist who rails against development in Florida, then resorts to terrorism to stop the growth. More bestsellers followed, including *Double Whammy* and *Skin Tight*. While Hiaasen continued to write his column, he spent less and less time in the *Herald*

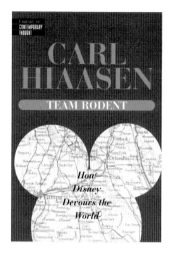

While most of Hiaasen's books are fiction, *Team Rodent* is a scathing take on the Disney empire. *Courtesy University Press of Florida.*

newsroom and more at home writing books—three columns a week became one column a week.

His book *Striptease* became an unsuccessful movie. One reviewer wrote that the movie was a "muddled and dumbed-down adaptation of Carl Hiaasen's bitingly funny book." It did produce a great movie poster featuring Demi Moore.

He moved to Islamorada in the Florida Keys, then to Vero Beach.

Writing in Florida, Hiaasen is blessed. Like Damon Runyon and Edna Buchanan, he is helped by the facts of life in Florida to keep his writing fresh. Any time a writer in Florida gets writer's block, there is certain to be a body washing up on shore, a politician caught in a cheap motel with someone other than his spouse or a scam so bizarre it inspires a writer.

Hiaasen was more than a keen observer of Florida politics and people, and he joined John D. MacDonald as an environmental writer. His books featured a subplot involving the threat to the Florida environment.

His columns railed at the destruction of Florida's environment, and two of his books were nonfiction collections of his columns, including *Paradise Screwed*. His book *Team Rodent: How Disney Devours the World* is a scathing series of articles on Disney's influence on the world.

In 1995, Hiaasen wrote an article for *Sports Illustrated* about the decline of Florida Bay, located at the tip of Florida.

In *Double Whammy*, he writes about a sleazy condo development built on a toxic waste dump. It is typical Hiaasen: A sleazy development is backed by forces bent on destroying the environment. Hiaasen's pages are packed by quick-buck operators. In *Double Whammy*, he contrasts the fate of land overrun by developers with the beauty of the nearby Everglades, but in between the lines, it is easy to see the fate that awaits the land. In 2021, he stopped writing his *Herald* column.

RANDY WAYNE WHITE

Randy Wayne White was born on a farm in Ohio and later moved to Iowa, where he graduated from high school in Davenport. In high school, he discovered John Steinbeck, Mark Twain and Arthur Conan Doyle. "I loved books, and I grew up reading."

After high school, he hit the road, traveling the country and even trying out for the Cincinnati Reds. After wandering for four years, he took a job with the *Fort Myers News-Press*. While working for the newspaper, he obtained his captain's license and began a thirteen-year career as a fishing guide, until the federal government closed Tarpon Bay to powerboats.

"The federal government decided to close our bay to powerboat traffic—permanently. I was out of a job. Worse, I wasn't qualified to do anything but drive a boat." White returned to writing, starting as a columnist for *Outside* magazine.

Using an old Underwood typewriter, he wrote columns on everything from Cuban refugees to working out with a Navy SEAL team. A publisher approached White to write a series of novels under the pen name Randy Striker. The publisher chose the characters and the format, and White did the writing.

In 1990, he created a series and characters, led by Doc Ford who lives on Sanibel Island—as White does. The book, *Sanibel Flats*, was the first in a successful series of more than two dozen books.

Ford is a marine biologist who is called on to rescue an eight-year-old boy who is being held prisoner in Central America. Ford rescues the boy and returns to his quiet life in Sanibel to await another adventure. White also created the Hannah Smith series and the Dusky MacMorgan books. Smith is a fishing guide and part-time investigator, while MacMorgan is a former Navy SEAL who works as a fisherman—like White—whose family is killed by drug runners. MacMorgan is ruthless in getting revenge.

A newspaper said, "When it comes to creating push-the-limits plots and loathsome bad guys," White excels. White has also written nonfiction books on his favorite subject, the outdoors. He has written two books on cooking and opened a chain of Doc Ford restaurants in Southwest Florida.

MICHAEL CONNELLY

Michael Connelly moved to Florida from Philadelphia when he was twelve years old. His father loved mystery books and shared his books with his son. At the University of Florida, he majored in construction until he discovered Raymond Chandler's books and switched to journalism and creative writing. One of Connelly's teachers was Harry Crews, who already had a national reputation for his writing.

After graduation, he worked for the *Daytona Beach News-Journal* and the *Fort Lauderdale Sun-Sentinel*, where he was a finalist for the Pulitzer Prize. He covered the police beat in a city with plenty of drugs and murders. His work drew the attention of the *Los Angeles Times*, which hired him to cover police there. Los Angeles was the city where Chandler wrote his bestselling mysteries.

Connelly began working on a novel, drawing from the crime stories he had covered. This book, featuring the lead character Hieronymus "Harry" Bosch, was *The Black Echo*, which brought him an Edgar Award for Best First Novel from the Mystery Writers of America. *Bosch* became a popular television series.

Bosch is a homicide detective who is named after the fifteenth-century Dutch artist Hieronymus Bosch. The literary Bosch's mother was a Hollywood prostitute who was murdered, and he spent his childhood in orphanages and juvenile facilities.

The book brought Connelly national recognition, and his follow-up books were huge bestsellers. After four books, Connelly quit his newspaper job to concentrate on books. His novel *Blood Work* became a movie starring Clint Eastwood, and he helped create the television series *Level 9*. His book *Lincoln Lawyer* became a movie starring Matthew McConaughey. Connelly has sold more than sixty million books, including editions in thirty-nine foreign languages.

CRAIG PITTMAN

Craig Pittman is one of the authors using his writing to sound the alarm about the environmental dangers Florida is facing. *Courtesy Craig Pittman.*

Craig Pittman's passion is the Florida environment. Like Carl Hiaasen, Pittman has sounded the alarm about what is happening to the Florida they both love.

And like Hiaasen, Pittman is a Florida native, born in Pensacola. He spent three decades at the *Tampa Bay Times*, ending his career there as a columnist with a focus on the environment.

While John D. MacDonald's books are fiction, Pittman fights the same battle with nonfiction books. His first book was *Manatee Insanity*, tracing the threat to the endangered manatee. Another book, *Cat Tale: The Wild, Weird Battle to Save the Florida Panther*, examined the threat to another Florida creature. *Scent of Scandal*, a nonfiction mystery about greed, smuggling and a beautiful orchid, remains a classic.

Pittman's book about how Florida is different from the other forty-nine states, *Oh, Florida: How America's Weirdest State Influences the Rest of the Country*, climbed the bestseller lists. After leaving the *Tampa Bay Times*, he joined the *Florida Phoenix* covering environmental issues.

TIM DORSEY

Tim Dorsey grew up in Riviera Beach, and after graduating from Auburn University, he returned to Florida to work for the *Tampa Tribune*. He was working as a copy editor for the *Tribune* when he wrote his first book in 1999. "I didn't tell anybody about it. I was afraid I'd jinx it. Finally, the book editor at the *Trib* got the fall catalog from the publisher, and my book was in it."

His first book was *Florida Roadkill*, which is set in Florida in 1997 as the Florida Marlins win the World Series. He created the psychopath Serge Storms, whose mental illness includes schizophrenia. He is an antihero in Dorsey's book, with a strong sense of right and wrong. His sidekick is Coleman, a drunk.

Serge finds creative ways to kill his enemies. In one book, he makes a mugger swallow bullets, then puts him in an MRI machine. The result is a corpse with exit wounds, but no entry wounds. In another, tire sealant is used to suffocate a victim.

Tim Dorsey created the psychopath
Serge Storms as his antihero.
Courtesy Tim Dorsey.

Dorsey is also a lover of Florida history, and his books take Serge to state
historic sites.

Dorsey weaves in the craziness of Florida into his books. In *Atomic Lobster*,
he features a Florida neighborhood full of degenerates, con men and what
are described as "prescription-abusing retirees in Buicks tying up traffic."

By 2020, "Florida Man" had become known throughout the world, but
surely Dorsey could claim part of the credit for creating Florida Man. No
matter how outrageous his characters—or his methods of disposing of
them—they all seem possible in Florida.

THE REAL FLORIDA

MARJORIE RAWLINGS

To her friends in Rochester, the decision by Marjorie Rawlings and her husband, Charles, to move to a rural crossroads in Florida must have left them shaking their heads. Marjorie was a successful writer for the *Rochester Evening Journal*, Rochester was a thriving city—home to Kodak—and she had only lived in cities.

She was born in Washington, D.C., in 1896; her father worked in the government patent office. She was just fourteen when she began writing, contributing letters and short stories to the *Washington Post*. At the University of Wisconsin, she met her future husband, Charles Rawlings. She worked as a writer for the YWCA for two years, and then the couple moved to Rochester, where they failed to find good jobs. She worked at the *Louisville Courier-Journal* until positions opened up in Rochester. She became a columnist, producing a column called "Songs of a Housewife," which was soon syndicated in fifty newspapers.

Her career seemed assured when they moved to Cross Creek, a tiny community south of Gainesville. She described it as a "primitive section off the beaten path, where men hunted and fished and worked small groves and farms for a meager living."

They purchased a small frame house and started their new lives. Charles could not adjust; it was not what he imagined, and he haunted the bars and beaches and disappeared for weeks at a time.

Marjorie Kinnan Rawlings often wrote on a table in front of her Cross Creek home. *Florida Archives.*

Her article "Cracker Childlings" appeared in *Scribner's Magazine* in 1931, capturing the flavor of her neighbors and surroundings. The article drew fans, including F. Scott Fitzgerald, Ernest Hemingway and Thomas Wolfe. The nation's leading book editor, Maxwell Perkins, was impressed and agreed to become her editor.

The story she titled "Gal Young 'Un" was to have been her first novel. Charles Scribner & Sons rejected it as "man-hating" and bitter because it dealt with her marriage difficulties. But *Harper's Magazine* turned it into a short story that won the O. Henry Prize in 1932.

The couple divorced in 1933, ending what Marjorie called "fourteen years of hell," but she feared what would come next. "I could have been a slave to a man who could be at least a benevolent despot."

Her first published novel was *South Moon Under*, the story of a young man who supports his wife by making moonshine, only to be betrayed to federal agents by a cousin. It was a fictional recounting of what had happened to her neighbors. It was a selection of the Book of the Month Club and a finalist for the Pulitzer Prize. A second, less successful book followed, but in 1938 she published her classic *The Yearling* to wide acclaim. This time she won the Pulitzer Prize, and Hollywood studios fought over the movie rights.

The book is filled with real people, friends and neighbors who lived in Cross Creek. These were people who taught her how to fish and hunt and how to make moonshine. The reactions to her book varied, although all were surprised to find their lives captured in her pages. A few were angered—one mother recognized her son in the book and threatened to take a whip to Rawlings. One neighbor and friend, Zelma Cason, filed suit claiming that Rawlings had invaded her privacy. The court battle dragged on for five years, and in the end, Cason won a one-dollar judgment.

The court battle drained Rawlings and ended her desire to write about her neighbors, and her writing declined. In 1940, she married Norton Baskin, who managed a hotel in St. Augustine that he owned with Rawlings.

In Jim Crow Florida, Rawlings developed a friendship with Zora Neale Hurston, and the two met often in St. Augustine and Cross Creek. Hurston dedicated one of her books to Rawlings. She was also friends with Ernest Hemingway, and the two met for drinks near St. Augustine. On December 13, 1953, Rawlings suffered a ruptured aneurysm and died the following day.

TOTCH BROWN

If there was anyone who epitomized the term *Florida cracker*, it was Loren "Totch" Brown. He wrote just one book, *Totch: A Life in the Everglades*, and it became a classic.

Brown's grandfather came to Florida in the 1800s, settling in the Everglades. When he arrived, civilization ended at Kissimmee two hundred miles to the north.

Totch got his first name and his nickname from a friend of his parents. From childhood, he was taught to hunt and fish. He dropped out of school when he was thirteen to help support his family amid the Great Depression. By the time he was seventeen, he was a commercial fisherman. He wrote, "The first settlers had but few choices on how to go about making a living. In the winter months, they hunted for raccoons and pretty much the year around for alligators."

The people of the area—on the southern tip of West Florida—were a tough lot. Many were escaping life in the North, avoiding either financial obligations or the police. Totch himself became one of the lawbreakers,

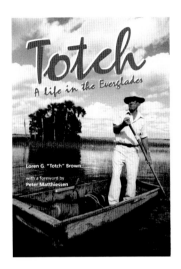

Totch Brown wrote just one book, but it became a classic about life in old Florida. *Courtesy University Press of Florida.*

ignoring the creation of the Everglades National Park, where he poached gators despite the federal prohibition.

He served in World War II, winning a Bronze Star at the Battle of the Bulge, then returned and increased his criminal activity, smuggling marijuana through the swamps. It brought him easy money, and soon he was leading a major drug organization. He brought drugs from Colombia to the South Florida swamps.

The federal government grew suspicious of his lifestyle, and he went to prison for income tax evasion.

Late in life, Totch wrote his book, and the University Press of Florida published it when he was seventy-three. Just as Patrick Smith, author of *A Land Remembered*, captured life in Florida before the crush of people, air conditioning and coastal resorts, Brown captured a bygone era known to only a few. It met with critical acclaim, and Brown might have written more, but he died in 1996.

HARRY CREWS

When Harry Crews died in 2012, the obituary in the *New York Times* said, "A Georgia-born Rabelais [François Rabelais was a French Renaissance writer known for satire], Mr. Crews was renowned for darkly comic bitingly satirical, grotesquely populated and almost preternaturally violent novels."

Crews was born in Georgia and experienced a childhood filled with horrors. His family was poor, and he once wrote, "There wasn't enough cash money in the county to close up a dead man's eyes." He said people ate clay for the nutrients it contained.

In his memoir, *A Childhood: The Biography of a Place*, Crews wrote, "Nearly everybody I knew had something missing, a finger cut off, a toe split, an ear half-chewed away, an eye clouded with blindness from a glancing fence staple. And if they didn't have something missing, they were carrying scars from barbed wire, or knives, or fishhooks."

Harry Crews was sent by *Playboy* magazine to interview actor Charles Bronson while he was filming *Heartbreak Pass. Author's collection.*

His father died when he was two, and his mother remarried his father's brother, a violent alcoholic. Crews himself became a legendary alcoholic before giving up liquor in the 1980s.

His father and stepfather were tenant farmers, and he lived in shacks with holes in the roof and the floor. At seventeen, he escaped to the Marines, serving during the Korean War. After his discharge, there were stints as a boxer, bouncer and sideshow barker. The jobs introduced him to the characters who would populate his books.

Using the GI Bill benefits, Crews enrolled at the University of Florida, but he soon dropped out to travel, then returned and graduated. He taught briefly at a Jacksonville elementary school then returned to the university to pursue a master's degree in creative writing. The university turned him down for admission, and he began teaching at Broward Community College.

In 1963, he published his first story, "The Unattached Smile," in the *Sewanee Review*, a respected literary journal. In 1968, he published his first novel, *The Gospel Singer.* It was the first of a string of books featuring hard-drinking brawlers with a long list of shortcomings. There was an occasional sociopath, a sideshow freak and a character who ate a 1971 Ford Maverick.

His book *The Hawk Is Dying* features a man who deals with condescension from college professors, much as Crews did. The main character's son drowns in the book, something Crews endured in real life. In 1964, his son Patrick drowned in a neighbor's pool, despite efforts by Crews to save him with mouth-to-mouth resuscitation.

Crews knew his books were dark and told those who asked why he didn't write anything more upbeat, "Listen, if you want to write about all sweetness and light and that stuff go get a job at Hallmark."

BREAKING NEW GROUND

JACK KEROUAC

Jack Kerouac was unknown and broke when he stepped off the bus from New York to Winter Park in 1956. He did not know that he would soon be joining the ranks of the literary elite, proclaimed as a new breed of writer.

He came in response to a plea from his mother, Gabrielle, who wanted her family reunited. Gabrielle, along with her daughter, Caroline, and son-in-law, moved to Florida hoping to cash in on the space boom then beginning in Florida.

Kerouac remained only a few weeks, then returned in 1957 when he and his mother moved into an apartment at the rear of a small house in Orlando's College Park neighborhood—which has no college, but a series of streets named for colleges.

He wrote *On the Road* in 1951 but failed to find a publisher. When the book was finally published two months after he arrived in Orlando, he became an instant celebrity. The *New York Times* called it "the most beautifully executed, the clearest and the most important utterance yet made by the generation Kerouac himself named years ago as 'beat' and whose principal avatar he is." The praise was not universal. Truman Capote said, "It isn't writing at all, it's typing."

The book was about his life on the road with fellow writers Allen Ginsberg and Neal Cassady (the publisher, Viking, forced Kerouac to change their names), in post–World War II America.

Jack Kerouac came to Florida at the urging of his mother just as he was about to become famous. *Library of Congress.*

Kerouac became a sensation, and perhaps it was best he was in the small town of Orlando. If he had stayed in New York, he would have been unable to resist the pressures and lures of the big city.

As he was being hailed, he sat in the backroom of a ramshackle house and typed away on his new project—*The Dharma Bums.* As with *On the Road*, he shunned conventional typewriter paper and used a large roll of yellow paper primarily used by the Associated Press and United Press for their teletype machines.

Neighbors in the quiet neighborhood could hear the typewriter keys clanking long into the night. *The Dharma Bums* was a poor follow-up.

Kerouac began moving between Florida and New York. His mother, who desperately wanted the family together, pulled him back to Florida time and again.

He bought land in the Orlando suburbs and planned to build a house for the entire family—his mother, sister and brother-in-law. As with so many things in Kerouac's life, nothing came of his plan. By 1964, relations with his sister, Caroline, had soured, and instead of returning to Orlando, he moved to St. Petersburg.

The downward spiral began. Sales of *On the Road* slowed, and Kerouac's third novel, *The Big Sur*, was even more of a flop than *The Dharma Bums*.

His name was still well known, and magazines purchased his work more to enhance their covers with his name than provide good writing for the readers. Despite large checks from *Playboy* and *Holiday*, he struggled to pay his bills.

Kerouac lived in this home in Orlando, where he wrote *The Dharma Bums* on the back porch. *Courtesy Jack Kerouac House.*

In Orlando, his sister's marriage fell apart, and she turned to Kerouac for money. He tried to help, remembering that his sister had been the one to bail him out when he was drunk. Shortly after moving to St. Petersburg, his sister died.

He was overcome with grief, telling friends he had berated her for failing to repay his loans, and the last time he saw her, in 1963, he was drunk and angry and she called police. "The last time I saw her I gave her hell," he wrote.

In St. Petersburg, he wrote *Desolation Angels*, an autobiography he had begun working on years before. Although called a novel, it was largely nonfiction, featuring stories about his friends and using thinly veiled names. The *New York Times* wrote, "The disaster is general," and "another bad book."

It was a strange life in St. Petersburg. While he struggled to pay his bills and reclaim his past literary glory, he became a tourist attraction. People—usually college students—came by the house at all hours to visit the famous writer, although he complained they usually scared his cat.

To escape the constant interruptions, he and his mother moved to Massachusetts, where he married an old friend, Stella Sampas, and began drinking heavily. "I'm so busy and drunk too all the time, and befuddled," he wrote to a friend.

The experiment in Massachusetts failed, and at his mother's urging, he went back to Florida—for the final time. His mother was ill, and she said, "I know if I get in that Florida sunshine I'll feel better."

In St. Petersburg, Kerouac's drinking intensified, and despite the presence of his wife and mother, he was increasingly lonely, reaching out to friends in after-midnight telephone calls.

He tried to write—considered writing another autobiography—and worked on old, unfinished projects.

On October 20, 1969, he began throwing up blood and called a friend for help. When the friend arrived, Kerouac blamed bad tuna for his condition, but the friend was alarmed and called an ambulance.

At the hospital, a nurse was shocked to learn he was only forty-seven. "He looked terrible. I thought he was much older," she said.

He was too weak for desperately needed surgery. He received repeated transfusions to build his strength without success. Doctors knew he was still weak, but the next morning they decided they could not wait any longer to repair the veins in his abdomen. As soon as they began the operation, they noticed the extensive damage. He died later in the afternoon.

He left a few thousand dollars, not enough to ship his body to New England for burial, but his estate became valuable nearly forty years later. The large roll of yellow paper he used to type *On the Road* was sold for $2.5 million to Jim Irsay, the owner of the Indianapolis Colts.

HUNTER THOMPSON

Hunter Thompson came to Florida with his dreams already shattered. He joined the Air Force with hopes of becoming a pilot, but his application for pilot training was rejected and he ended up at Elgin Air Force Base in the Florida Panhandle, not far from the Alabama border. Some of his friends ended up in the Arctic Circle, so he counted himself fortunate.

Thompson and the Air Force were a bad fit—he once threw a liquor bottle at a camp guard, but things improved when he found that Florida State University offered night classes on the base. He signed up for a literature course and soon became friends with the program director.

Thompson embellished his background—perhaps *embellish* is too kind a word for the tales Thompson told—and he landed a job as sports editor of the base newspaper, the *Command Courier*. His lack of qualifications became clear; his spelling was terrible, and he seemed to have had a basic lack of understanding of the English language.

One of his assignments was to cover the base football team, which that year was far from routine. It featured two members of the Green Bay Packers, Max McGee and Zeke Bratkowski, and briefly a future member of the Packers, Bart Starr. Thompson got to travel with the team as it piled up victories—including one over Rutgers.

Despite his shortcomings as a writer, Thompson parlayed his work on the camp newspaper into a part-time job on the Fort Walton Beach newspaper, the *Playground Daily News.* He wrote under pen names because his work violated Air Force policy—hardly anything new for Thompson.

He clashed frequently with his Air Force superiors and could not deal with authority figures. The Air Force wanted Thompson gone, and he wanted to leave, but not with a dishonorable discharge. A compromise was reached, and Thompson was allowed to leave with his honorable discharge.

His limited experience was enough to land him a job as a sports editor at a small Pennsylvania newspaper. He moved to New York—where *Time* magazine fired him from his copy clerk job for insubordination—and finally he ended up in San Francisco, where the hippie culture was flourishing.

He returned to Florida in the late 1960s as a well-known writer based on his adventures with the Hells Angels.

He became a sometime resident of Key West, which he said was "where the weird go pro." There he was joined by Laila Nabulsi, who would later produce a movie based on his book *Fear and Loathing in Las Vegas.* The two walked the streets of the town carrying a bullhorn to broadcast absurd warnings and drove through town in his Buick convertible shouting for pedestrians to get out of the way.

He fell in with some of the island's most famous residents: Jimmy Buffett, Thomas McGuane, painter Russell Chapman and Paul Schrader.

Schrader wrote *Taxi Driver* and was in town to write *Raging Bull.* Thompson was desperate for money—a chronic state—and thought screenwriting would be a path to fortune. Shrader gave tips to McGuane, who was turning *Ninety-Two in the Shade* into a movie.

Thompson picked drug smuggling in Key West as his topic—something he was familiar with—and sold the idea to Paramount Pictures. He called it *Cigarette Key* and set out to write a script in Buffett's apartment. Thompson was no screenwriter, and when Paramount Pictures saw the work, the studio killed the project.

He wrote a couple of magazine pieces in Key West, one on the Mariel boatlift, the other on treasure hunter Mel Fisher. By then, he had become known as the founder of gonzo journalism, an uncertain term used to describe a writing form where the writer plays a role in the story and objectivity is often discarded. The name comes from an article Thompson wrote, "The Gonzo Salvage Company," about treasure hunting in the Keys.

In 1986, he returned to Key West with the type of idea only Thompson could come up with. He created a television show—he thought it might be a morning program—starring himself. The crew stayed in Thompson's favorite motel, the Sugar Loaf Lodge on Sugar Loaf Key, but making a television program was hard work involving long days and many retakes. Thompson's day began at noon, and even then, work was difficult for him. After a week, they had only two hours of film, and like so many, another Thompson scheme failed.

On February 20, 2005, Thompson was at his home in Colorado when he put a .455-caliber automatic into his mouth and pulled the trigger.

DISTINGUISHED TOURISTS

NED BUNTLINE

Ned Buntline is known for creating the dime novel, turning western lawmen into heroes for millions of readers. His real name was Edward Judson, and he first came to public notice when he saved drowning people in New York's East River. He was honored by President Martin Van Buren, who gave him a navy commission at the age of sixteen.

The commission brought him to Florida, where he served in the Florida Keys during the Second Seminole War. He adopted a nautical name—a buntline is a rope attached to haul up the sail. He was executive officer on the *Otsego*, which patrolled the coast.

Although he made his reputation with western novels, he began his writing in Florida. Buntline was the first popular writer to come to Florida and utilize the scenic backdrop and Indian wars. In Buntline's writing, Florida was an exciting place, and his earliest dime novels were set in Florida, although they did not sell as well as his western novels would in later years.

His stories included "A Cruise in Lake Okeechobee," "A Chase in the Everglades," "The Capture and Trial" and "Indian Key: Its Rise, Progress and Destruction." His Florida books included *Matanzas; or, A Brother's Revenge*. It sold well, even though it was just forty-six pages long.

He started a series of magazines, which all failed, and entered a series of marriages, which also failed.

He finally found fame when he wrote a story about Buffalo Bill Cody for *New York Weekly*, "Buffalo Bill the King of the Border Men." It was largely fictional but became a bestseller and set the pattern for hundreds of books to follow. The "novels" cost a dime each and gave readers an adventure story, making a hero of someone who may or may not have earned the title.

One of his longest books, *The White Wizard, or, The Great Prophet of the Seminoles*, which he wrote in 1858, was originally written for the *New York Mercury*, then later as a book. As he did with his western books, he often used real people, then fictionalized their lives. Although he left Florida, he still loved it. "I love a Florida winter. I do not mean one of your northern winter evenings, only rendered clear through the intense frigidity of the stiffened atmosphere. I allude to one where the bright-faced moon and dancing stars look down on forests clothed in the rich beauty of perennial greenness, on an earth covered with luscious, air-perfuming fruit."

SIDNEY LANIER

Sidney Lanier had his entire life planned. He would study in Germany, then embark on a career as a writer. The Civil War changed his plans and his life. He was taken prisoner while serving on a blockade runner off the Virginia coast, and his health was ruined in a Union prison camp. When the war ended, Lanier had just sixteen years to live.

He came to Florida in 1875 at the invitation of the Atlantic Coast Line Railway, which hired him to write a guidebook of Florida to lure customers for the railroad. As thousands of poets have found, making money from poetry is difficult, and Lanier was happy to lend his name and writing ability to help promote the railroad.

He and his wife left their children in Philadelphia and headed for Florida. He arrived in the spring, setting up an office in Jacksonville, and spent three months traveling to different parts of the state. Although he wrote about Key West and South Florida, it is doubtful that he went that far south—a railroad would not come within one hundred miles of Miami for another two decades.

Lanier stressed the health benefits of spending time in Florida. Doctors were recommending the state's warm climate for patients suffering from what was then known as consumption, which included tuberculosis and other lung-related ailments. Lanier's doctors thought Florida would help his lung ailments.

In Tampa, the wife of the editor of the *Tampa Sunland Tribune* sent him a jar of marmalade, and he responded with a verse:

> *How oft the answers to our passing prayers*
> *Drop down in forms our fancy ne'er foretold!*
> *Thus when of late, consumed by wasting cares,*
> *"Angels preserve us" from my lips up rolled,*
> *I'm sure I pictured not—as thus I prayed—*
> *Angels preserving me—with marmalade!!!*

Lanier's health improved, and he began riding horseback daily and writing regularly, turning out nearly ten poems in the three months. To many in Tampa. Lanier was more popular as a musician than a poet. He performed for a local club and earned accolades as the "finest flutist of the South."

The *Tribune* noted the Laniers' departure in April 1877: "They leave many warm friends behind them, and they will be sadly missed in the community."

The result was *Florida: Its Scenery, Climate, and History*, which has little literary merit but did put $125 in Lanier's pocket. Lanier's improvement proved only temporary, and in 1881, he died of tuberculosis at the age of thirty-nine.

WILLIAM DEAN HOWELLS

William Dean Howells became known as the "Dean of American Letters" for his writing and novels, including *The Rise of Silas Lapham*.

Howells was born in Ohio, where his father was a newspaper editor. During the 1860 presidential campaign, the younger Howells wrote a positive biography of Lincoln and was rewarded with a diplomatic post. He became acquainted with St. Augustine through his friend Constance Woolson, who wrote an article about the city for *Harper's Monthly Magazine*.

Within a few weeks in 1910, his friend Mary Twain died and his wife passed away. Howells was alone in a home he called "dreadful in its ghostliness and ghastliness."

In 1912, his brother Joseph, in failing health, moved to Auburndale, a small village in Central Florida. William came to Florida, after trying to visit Bermuda in 1914, only to be frightened off by German submarines in the area. California was rejected because it was so far away, and Panama was also rejected. "We have given up Panama and are thinking much less boldly of St. Augustine." His oculist (now known as an ophthalmologist) had moved there, and his barber highly recommended it.

Howells checked in at the Alcazar Hotel, then moved to less expensive lodging at the Valencia Hotel. When he returned to New York, he wrote a two-part article for *Harper's* titled, "A Confession of St. Augustine."

"The charm is very complex, as a true charm always is, but the place is very simple." He pointed out that the heyday was between the 1870s and 1880s. The great freeze struck, and "then the summer shores of Palm Beach and Miami took the primacy from California, and Florida was again the desire of our winter travel and sojourn."

By the time Howells arrived, St. Augustine was in decline, as the wealthy headed for Ormond Beach, Palm Beach and even Miami.

HENRY JAMES

Henry James was born in New York City and spent much of his life traveling the world, studying and writing. On a visit to Europe in the 1870s, he wrote his first novel, *Roderick Hudson*. He settled in Paris, where he wrote *The Americans*, which attracted international attention.

By 1879, he was living in London when he wrote *Daisy Miller*, a classic. Over the next two decades, he wrote *Washington Square*, *The Portrait of a Lady*, *The Turn of the Screw* and *The Ambassadors*.

He returned to the United States in 1904 with an idea to write a series of essays about life in America. His tour included his old haunts in New England, as well as places that had not existed the last time he was in the United States, such as Palm Beach.

To finance his journey, James planned to charge for his speeches—which he said were mostly to women's groups who were pleased to pay him large sums—and by writing magazine pieces. He said the women were willing to "pay through the nose" for one of his talks.

James may have planned a simple travel book, but it became the most controversial of his writings. He was shocked when he saw the changes in America that took place while he was in Europe.

He saw a nation captivated by materialism, was alarmed at the rising immigration rate and reflected the racial attitudes of the time. The final section of his book, *The American Scene*, bemoaned the environmental damage being done, the rising racial tensions and the overheated economic development. He wrote that the nation was doing a "devil's dance," and the nation's future was uncertain.

It was so alarmist that his American publishers, Harper & Brothers, omitted the final chapter about Palm Beach, although it appeared in the edition published in England. In the final chapter of his conflicted and controversial travelogue *The American Scene*, Henry James describes his 1905 trip to Palm Beach.

He was taken with "the velvet air, the color of the sea, the 'royal' palms, clustered here and there, and in the nobleness of beauty, their single sublime distinction, putting every other mark and sign to the blush."

At the time, the Breakers had been open for less than a year. Rebuilt after a 1903 fire, the four-story, 425-room Colonial building was a vision of luxury. (A third Breakers replaced it.) Regular visitors included the Astors, the Vanderbilts, J.P. Morgan and J.C. Penney. He called the hotel "vast and cool and fair, friendly, breezy, shiny, swabbed and burnished like a royal yacht, really immaculate and delightful." James dismissed the richest people in the world as "boarders" at two of the most expensive hotels in the nation, the Breakers and the Royal Poinciana—where James stayed. To him, they were just "hordes of humanity."

F. SCOTT FITZGERALD

In the 1920s, Florida was booming, and F. Scott Fitzgerald was the author whose work reflected the decade. In Florida, the wealthy flocked to resorts in Palm Beach and Miami, and Fitzgerald was there to write about the wealthy and those who aspired to be.

His first book, *This Side of Paradise*, came out at the beginning of the decade and began the chronicle of his generation. He and his wife, Zelda, lived recklessly, spending money faster than they made it.

He enjoyed the luxury of Palm Beach and the new Don CeSar Hotel on St. Petersburg Beach. The Don CeSar opened in 1928, just as the Florida land boom was turning into a bust. On a visit as the economy collapsed, he saw the problems:

> *The Don CeSar Hotel in Pass-A-Grille stretched lazily over the stubbed wilderness, surrendering its shape to the blinding brightness of the gulf. Opalescent shells capped the twilight on the beach and a stray dog's footprints in the wet sand staked out his claim to a free path round the ocean....The*

hotel was almost empty and there were so many waiters waiting to be off that we could hardly eat our meals.

The hotel provided relaxation, but Zelda's mental health remained fragile. She suffered from bipolar disorder and moved in and out of institutions. In 1932, while staying at the Don CeSar, Zelda suffered a breakdown and was rushed to the Phipps Psychiatric Clinic in Baltimore. Her husband took an apartment nearby, and during the four months she was hospitalized, he began work on *Tender Is the Night*. After her release, they returned to the Don CeSar, where he completed the book.

He wrote two stories centered in Florida. The first, *The Rich Boy*, is considered his finest novella. It deals with the gap between rich and poor, a constant theme of Fitzgerald's. The lead character, Anson Hunter, was modeled after his close friend and Princeton classmate Ludlow Fowler, to whom Fitzgerald wrote, "I have written a 15,000-word story about you called *The Rich Boy*—it is so disguised that no one except you and me and maybe two of the girls concerned would recognize, unless you give it away, but it is in large measure the story of your life, toned down here and there and simplified."

Fitzgerald wrote,

Palm Beach sprawled plump and opulent between the sparkling sapphire of Lake Worst, flawed here and there by houseboats at anchor, and the great turquoise bar of the Atlantic Ocean. The huge bulks of the Breakers and the Royal Poinciana rise as twin paunches from the bright level of the sand, and around them clustered the Dancing Glade, Bradley's House of Chance, and a dozen modistes and milliners with goods at triple prices from New York. Upon the trellised veranda of the Breakers two hundred women stepped right, stepped left, wheeled, and slid in that then celebrated calisthenic known as the double-shuffle, while in half-time to the music two thousand bracelets clicked up and down on two hundred arms.

He also wrote "The Offshore Pirate," for the *Saturday Evening Post* in 1920, and it was included in his first collection of short stories, *Flappers and Philosophers*. The story deals with a group of phony pirates who kidnap a wealthy woman onboard her yacht. There are twists, turns and a happy ending.

EDNA ST. VINCENT MILLAY

Would it have been her greatest work? No one will ever know.

Edna St. Vincent Millay was born in 1892 and won her first poetry prize while still in her teens. By 1920, her poems were appearing in *Vanity Fair*, and in 1923, she won the Pulitzer Prize for poetry, becoming known for her sonnets and public readings, which drew packed houses.

Millay was so popular that she made regular appearances on national radio programs, reciting her latest works.

In late 1935, she and her husband, Eugen Boissevain, decided to vacation in Florida, and her husband found a home in Delray Beach. They rented a fully furnished house, which came with everything except hot water. There was no water heater, just a tank on the roof heated by the sun. Millay complained that since the weather was cold and rainy, there was just cold water.

She spent her time working on the final revisions of a translation of the French poet Baudelaire and pushing herself to complete the final proofs. She was under pressure from Harper & Bros., which was rushing to publish the book. "It is obvious that Harper & Bros. are trying to kill us so that they'll never have to have anything to do with either of us again." She battled with the publisher over the cover and the title. She began mocking Harper and Brothers as Sharper and Smothers.

The book was finally published in April 1936, to mixed reviews. The *Saturday Review* slammed the book, while the *New York Times* called it "a magnificent translation." With the work completed, Millay turned to finish *Confessions at Midnight,* a series of poems based on a conversation between seven men on the eve of World War II.

On the first of May, she and her husband left Delray Beach for the drive back home. They wrote to friends that they hoped to be home on the eighth after a visit to Sanibel Island, a long drive on the other side of the state.

When they arrived at Sanibel at dusk, they were eager to start hunting for shells on the beach. They checked into the Palms Hotel, a ramshackle wooden structure, and headed to the beach.

As they began their walk, Eugen remembered that the manuscript for *Confessional of Midnight* was still under the front seat of the car. He left Millay on the beach and hurried back to fetch the manuscript and leave it in the hotel with the rest of their baggage.

As they walked, something caused Millay to turn around and she saw the hotel engulfed in flames. Nothing was saved, including her treasured emerald ring and a cherished seventeenth-century copy of poetry by Catullus, which she said was "the only thing that touched me emotionally, the only thing I mourned for."

Her husband wrote, "The terrible thing is, that Edna lost the entire Mss. of her new book, which was going to the printer in June—And the Mss. of practically another book—I hope she will be able to remember many of them—But the whole thing has shaken her up quite a bit, and she does not seem to wish to start trying to remember them."

They had only the clothes they were wearing on the beach and wore them during the days-long journey back home.

The task of re-creating *Confessions at Midnight* proved daunting. She wrote, "Under more favourable conditions, since I have a good memory, I might have been able to recall the whole book." She said that if there was some version of the manuscript to guide her, she could do it.

As Millay began re-creating her manuscript, she suffered a more serious tragedy. She was riding in a car when the door flew open, and she was hurled out and thrown down a rocky hill. The accident cause extensive nerve damage and she was never to know a day without pain. There were many surgeries and regular doses of morphine. Her husband wrote, "We certainly have had…bad luck this year!"

Eventually, *Conversations* was published, and it was far different from anything she had written. It is a play in poem form involving a late-night conversation among seven men with very different views on the state of the world.

The *New York Times Book Review* gave it front-page review, and it was an alternate selection of the Book of the Month Club. Generally, the reviews were favorable, although some of her friends, including Edmund Wilson, criticized it. What will never be known is how much of the original manuscript was lost as a result of the fire and the terrible auto accident.

In 1950, she suffered a heart attack and fell down a flight of stairs. Her body was found eight hours later.

Millay's memory of Florida centered on the struggle with Harper and Brothers and the burning of her manuscript. When she encountered friends later, they were unsure of what to say. Millay eased the mood by saying, "Oh, Florida. O, cold Florida! Could any state be horrida?"

NOVEMBER 1960

JOHN KENNEDY AND ROBERT FROST

The two men were preparing to speak before the largest audience of their lives. John Kennedy was working in Palm Beach while Robert Frost was a little more than an hour away in Coconut Grove.

It was strange that both men were in Florida since both were synonymous with New England. And the age difference could not have been more pronounced: Kennedy, about to take the presidential oath office, was forty-three years old, while Frost was twice that.

Despite the age difference, they had both begun coming to Florida in the 1930s, Kennedy, the son of one of the wealthiest families in America, Frost, the well-known poet.

Joseph Kennedy, one of the nation's wealthiest men, discovered Palm Beach in the 1930s, purchasing a beachfront mansion for family vacations and romantic meetings with his mistress, actress Gloria Swanson.

His children joined him frequently, although Joe and John were older and were infrequent visitors. It was not until after World War II that John Kennedy came to think of Palm Beach as a second home.

Within the Kennedy family, it was always thought that the first son, Joe, would be the politician. When Joe Kennedy died in the war, the mantle fell to John Kennedy.

Throughout his life, John Kennedy suffered a series of health problems, and injuries suffered in the war made them worse. He was hospitalized three dozen times during his life and given last rites three times.

His most serious problem was his back, which caused problems starting in the 1930s. He underwent his first back surgery in 1944, but problems persisted until his death.

In late 1954, he went to Palm Beach to recover from an operation and had time to think and write. His original idea was to write a series of magazine articles about U.S. senators he thought had shown unusual courage. As he drew up his list, he dropped his magazine idea and thought it would make a better book.

The book, *Profiles in Courage*, was published in early 1956 to positive reviews and tremendous sales, spending nearly two years on the bestseller list. In 1957, the book won the Pulitzer Prize for biography.

The book helped Kennedy's political career. In the Senate, he had been considered a lightweight. Majority Leader Lyndon Johnson referred to him as "that boy," and "Johnny." A bestseller and a Pulitzer Prize gave him instant credibility, especially among the journalists who covered politics and saw the Pulitzer Prize as the Holy Grail.

No sooner had the book been published than there was controversy over its publication, a controversy that lasted for half a century.

The first controversy was over the Pulitzer Prize, which turned out to have been awarded in strange circumstances. It was not one of the finalists but was pushed by a respected Pulitzer judge, *New York Times* columnist Arthur Krock. What no one knew was the close relationship between Joseph Kennedy Sr. and Krock. At times, Krock received payments from Kennedy. One historian found that the relationship "reveals something quite disturbing, if not corrupt, about Krock's willingness to do Kennedy's bidding, to advise him or write a speech for him, then praise it in his column."

There was also speculation about who wrote *Profiles in Courage*. Shortly after the book was published, columnist Drew Pearson was interviewed by Mike Wallace of ABC. "John F. Kennedy is the only man in history that I know who won a Pulitzer Prize for a book that was ghostwritten for him." Wallace said, "You know for a fact, Drew, that the book *Profiles in Courage* was written for Senator Kennedy?" Pearson said yes.

The Kennedy family responded by hiring one of Washington's most famous attorneys, Clark Clifford, who threatened to sue Pearson and Wallace, while Bobby Kennedy and his father went to ABC executives and showed them John Kennedy's notes for the book.

ABC, then the weakest of the three networks, backed down without a fight, and a week later, an ABC executive read a statement on national television apologizing.

Subsequent events support Pearson. Historian Herbert Parmet found that Kennedy was more of an overseer rather than an author. Kennedy came up with the idea and the structure and dictated many pages. It fell to his aide, Ted Sorenson, to do much of the writing, although others were involved, including Jules Davids of Georgetown University.

For half a century, Sorenson denied that he was the author; then in 2008, he published his memoirs and painted a true picture of what had happened. He wrote that Kennedy worked on the first and last chapters, but Sorenson wrote the first draft of most of the book. Sorenson also said over the years he had been paid generously by Kennedy and the Kennedy family to guarantee his silence.

The original plan for Frost and his wife, Elinor, was to winter in Miami after taking the train from New York. Even in the Great Depression, Frost found the prices too high. Elinor wrote to her daughter, "We have made enough inquiries today to find out rents anywhere in this region are way beyond our means." With family members in tow, they pushed on to Key West, which was affordable, but hardly a garden spot.

The city went bankrupt in 1934, and Julius Stone, the state director of the Federal Emergency Relief Administration, was sent in to salvage the situation and make services available. He ended up transforming the island into a tourist mecca.

Frost's complaints began almost immediately. "There is no sanitation. The water is all off the roofs and after it goes through people I don't know where it goes. Everything is shabby and even delipidated." (Key West did not get a reliable water system until World War II.) He said Key West "is a very, very dead place because it has died several times. It died as a resort of pirates, then as a house of smugglers and wreckers…then as a winter resort boomtown."

Elinor's views were even harsher. She found the town "strange and outlandish" and blamed the government's handling of the bankruptcy. Elinor, a major critic of the Roosevelt administration, called Stone a dictator and criticized his actions.

In February 1935, Frost encountered Wallace Stevens, who had been one of the first writers to come to Key West. For years, he had been *the* poet in Key West. Frost was far more famous, creating instant jealousy. Frost already had two Pulitzer Prizes, while Stevens was still two decades from winning his only Pulitzer Prize.

Frost accepted an invitation to join Stevens for dinner. As happened far too often, Stevens had too much to drink even before dinner. The two argued, and Frost was shocked by Stevens's condition.

When Robert Frost first viisited Key West, he found much to complain about, including the water system. *Key West Art and Historical Society.*

When Frost gave a speech at the University of Miami, he mentioned Stevens's drinking. Predictably, the speech got back to Stevens, and Frost apologized. Frost told others he did not like Stevens's poems.

Stevens was no longer the leading poet on the island, and rather than compete, he surrendered. "Key West is no longer quite the delightful affection it once was." Stevens never returned to Key West.

Years later, when Stevens was asked to attend Frost's eightieth birthday celebration at Amherst, he wrote, "I do not know his work well enough to be either impressed or unimpressed." It is hard to imagine any poet not knowing Frost's poetry.

Elinor was unhappy with the Key West schools and began homeschooling two of her grandchildren. She had no plans to return to Key West. "If we leave home for climate again, I think we should seek the Arizona desert."

Before returning to Florida, they spent winters in Arizona and Texas.

Elinor's health was failing; her heart was enlarged, and she underwent surgery to have her right breast removed. Frost was overcome, writing to her friend, "She has been the unspoken half of everything I ever wrote."

She recovered and wrote to her daughter, "Everything is going fine."

As winter approached, she and Frost decided to go to Gainesville with their daughter Lesley and her two little girls. They stayed in a hotel until they found two apartments in a large home. Elinor and Lesley had a prolonged argument over who should take the upstairs apartment. Strangely, for a woman with a serious heart condition, Elinor wanted the upstairs unit. It meant she would be climbing a flight of stairs several times a day

Elinor liked Gainesville more than Key West or Miami and readily agreed when Robert suggested buying a house. She was pleased that North Florida was more conservative than South Florida.

The entire family went on house-hunting expeditions and found a place they all liked on March 15, 1938. They returned to their apartment late in the afternoon after a long day, and as Elinor climbed the stairs, she suffered

Robert Frost build his home and called it *Pencil Pines. Author's collection.*

a heart attack. She said it was not serious, but Robert called a doctor, who said her condition was serious and she could not be moved. Hours later, she suffered another heart attack and slipped into a coma. Then came seven more attacks, and late Sunday afternoon, she died. Plans for the Gainesville house were dropped.

Today, the University of Miami is one of the most successful universities in the nation, but in the 1930s, the school struggled to overcome financial problems. Frost said the school was "wretched" and in desperate need of cash.

Frost was looking for a warm-weather base and a college where he could give lectures and find intellectual stimulation. The university was looking for someone to bring recognition and contributions.

Before he committed to Coconut Grove, he went to Key West. For several days, he walked the streets looking for a house, finding nothing appropriate.

In Coconut Grove, Frost found a five-acre lot he named Pencil Pines. He assembled a prefab house over several years and spent much of his time working in the yard, calling himself "a cross between a Florida farmer and a Vermont farmer." There was a New England touch; he ordered two prefabricated cottages from New England, which were put together by a local carpenter.

Frost never wrote poetry about Florida, but it is believed that it did influence the title of one of his collections. He changed the title of his 1961 book *The Great Misgiving* to *In the Clearing* as he recuperated at his home from pneumonia.

In the 1960 election, Frost supported his fellow New Englander John Kennedy, and Kennedy quoted from Frost's poem "Stopping by Woods on a Snowy Evening" dozens of times during the campaign: "But I have promises to keep, and miles to go before I sleep."

Frost was pleased when Stewart Udall was named secretary of the interior, and it was Udall who suggested that Frost play a role in the inauguration.

At first, Kennedy rejected the idea, thinking that Frost might upstage him. Once he accepted the idea, Kennedy asked Frost if he could write something new for the inauguration, but Frost declined. Turned down for his original plan, Kennedy asked Frost to read "The Gift Outright," which Frost described as "a history of the United States in a dozen [really sixteen] lines of blank verse."

> *The land was ours before we were the land's,*
> *She was our land more than a hundred years*
> *Before we were her people. She was ours*
> *In Massachusetts, in Virginia,*
> *But we were England's still colonials,*
> *Possessing what we still were unpossessed by,*
> *Possessed by what we now no more possessed…*

Frost did agree to Kennedy's request to change the final line from "Such as she was, such as she would become," to "such as she will become." Kennedy thought his change sounded more optimistic.

Frost wrote the poem in the 1930s but did not publish it until 1942. Even though he knew the poem by heart, he practiced reciting the poem many times in his Coconut Grove home.

Following the success of *Profiles in Courage*, Sorenson signed on as a Kennedy speechwriter and, after the election, began to work on the inaugural address. Kennedy spent much of his time between the November election and the January inauguration in Palm Beach, while Sorenson worked in Washington.

Frost wrote a special poem for the Kennedy Inauguration, but the weather ruined his plans. *Library of Congress.*

Around Christmas 1960, Kennedy began to concentrate on the speech. John Kennedy Galbraith visited Kennedy and brought an address he had written, and Kennedy sent telegrams to nearly a dozen others asking for input.

A week before the inauguration, Sorenson flew to Palm Beach; for the next week, they worked on the address, which included the line "Ask not what your country can do for you, ask what you can do for your country."

Exactly who inserted the line into the inauguration speech is unknown, but it is hardly original. Scholars have found similar quotes dating back to 1884, when Oliver Wendell Holmes Jr. said, "To recall what our country has done for us, and to ask ourselves what we can do for our country in return."

While Kennedy was putting the finishing touches on his part of the inaugural, seventy-five miles away Robert Frost was having second thoughts about his part in the ceremony. Perhaps Kennedy was right, and the occasion called for a poem written for the great event. He went to work on "Dedication," which was more topical. He wanted to recite "Dedication," followed by "The Gift Outright."

The eve of the inauguration brought a massive snowstorm and bitterly cold weather to Washington. Some questioned whether the outdoor event would even take place.

When Udall arrived at Frost's hotel room in Washington to take him to the inauguration, he was surprised to find the new plan. Frost had written the poem down but had not had time to memorize it.

> *Summoning artists to participate*
> *In the august occasions of the state*
> *Seems something ought to celebrate.*
> *Today is for my cause a day of days.*
> *And his be poetry's old-fashioned praise*
> *Who was the first to think of such a thing…*

About an hour into the ceremony, Frost rose and walked a few feet to the podium. He began to read "Dedication," but the bright sun was in his eyes, and the wind threatened to blow the manuscript away. Frost faltered, even though the new vice president, Lyndon Johnson, rose to block the sun with his hat.

He switched and began reciting "The Gift Outright" from memory. He did remember the closing line Kennedy requested. The applause was deafening, and no one noticed that Frost thanked "president-elect, Mr. John Finley."

Frost continued to come to Florida, although his visits were limited to about three months from January to March.

Kennedy was a frequent visitor to Palm Beach during his presidency and came the final week of his life. He arrived on Friday, November 15, with just a week to live. The next morning, he took off for Cape Canaveral to track the course of the space programs and watch a Polaris missile fired from a submarine. He flew to Tampa for a speech to a union group, then to Miami for a rally and dinner speech. That night, he returned to Washington. His calendar showed that he planned to come back at Christmas.

THE KEYS

ZANE GREY

By 1911, the decline of the Florida Keys was well underway. Most of the Keys were nearly empty, while Key West suffered the most from poverty. To the north, Miami was just fifteen years old and had only five thousand people.

That was when Zane Grey arrived in Long Key, about sixty miles north of Key West. Grey was certainly more famous than the Key he visited by accident.

Grey struggled early in his career, until 1910, when he published *The Heritage of the Desert*, which became a bestseller. He loved to travel and fish and usually combined the two. With the success of his book, he set off for a fishing vacation in Tampico, Mexico, stopping in Cuba, where he learned there was a smallpox outbreak in Tampico. He headed for the Bahamas, finding the fishing poor, but got a tip about the great fishing in Long Key.

Long Key was home to two coconut plantations until Henry Flagler's Florida East Coast Railway came through bringing hundreds of workers, followed by tourists. He built a seventy-five-room hotel and a general store. At first, Grey was unimpressed, writing, "There is absolutely nothing to do here when you can't fish. It is only a barren strip of island." His opinion changed, and he wrote an article for *Field and Stream* titled, "The Sea-Tigers of the Florida Keys," which made Long Key look like the fishing capital of the world. "Long Key is a place to thrill and to invite one's soul."

Zane Grey and his brother, R.C., show their catch of the day on Long Key in 1916. *Florida Archives.*

When he returned in 1912, he found that his article had inspired a rise in tourism. This time the weather was bad, and he could fish for just three days. While he waited for the weather to clear, he learned that his new book, *Riders of the Purple Sage*, was drawing bad reviews. The book would go on to be a bestselling classic and lead to five movie versions, but the critics' reaction left him depressed.

The prime catch was the kingfish, which was plentiful off the Key. The fish no one wanted to catch was the sailfish—nicknamed "boohoo," by fishermen. They complained that they could not catch the kingfish because there were only sailfish.

Grey changed that, making the sailfish one of the popular catches. In 1919, he wrote a pamphlet, *Tales of Fishes*, which introduced what became known as Gulfstream fishing. Grey called the maligned sailfish "the gamest, most beautiful and spectacular and the hardest fish to catch on light tackle."

Like Hemingway two decades later, Grey rose early and wrote for several hours before heading out to sea. Grey spent eight to ten hours with his guide, Bill Partea, then returned to his room about 10:00 p.m. to write some more. For thirteen of the next fifteen years, it was a pattern he followed when the weather permitted.

One of the books he wrote in Long Key was *The Light of the Western Stars*, which became a silent movie in 1918 and was remade in 1940 starring Victor Jory, Alan Ladd and Noah Beery Jr.

Grey became famous throughout the world, and his fame brought tourists to Florida. He helped start the Long Key Fishing Club in 1916 and became its first president. Herbert Hoover and Franklin Roosevelt became members of the club, which recommended catch and release.

In 1924, Grey wrote *Tales of Southern Rivers*, which was far different from the western adventure stories his readers were used to. He considered the Gulf Stream a river, flowing from the Gulf of Mexico through the Keys and up the east coast of Florida. "The sea, from which all life springs, has been equally with the desert my teacher and religion."

He proved to be too successful in promoting the Keys, and as tourism increased, he became less enamored with the attraction he had played a role in creating. Other places, and other women, drew him away. The solitude he had found in Long Key was gone.

JOHN DOS PASSOS

Today, Key West is a thriving mecca, spawning its own lifestyle and earning the nickname the Conch Republic. In the 1920s, it had fallen on hard times. For more than three hundred years, Key West thrived as a home for men who made their fortunes salvaging ships sunk by pirates or storms.

To subdue the pirates, the U.S. Navy established a base in 1832. In the 1830s, Key West was the most important part of the richest county in the nation. The Spanish-American War brought a surge of money flowing into the island, and World War I brought military airplanes there.

The sprawling Fort Zachary Taylor saw small numbers of soldiers come and go but was outdated before it was completed. Otherwise, there was little to recommend the island—there was no water supply, and the economy was in tatters. With the end of World War I, the base was closed and remained shut for two decades.

The island was in decline when John Dos Passos arrived after stops in Baltimore; Washington, D.C.; Savannah; and New Orleans. As he traveled, he worked on his book *Manhattan Transfer*, his breakthrough novel about life in New York City spanning the late 1800s and early 1900s.

In Florida, Dos Passos found what he had been seeking. He arrived during a building boom. In Palm Beach, he found the new winter playground for the rich and powerful and wrote that Florida was "fabulous and movie-like."

As he watched the boom, he wrote tongue in cheek to his French friend Germaine Lucas-Championnière, "One arrives on foot, works a year, buys an orange grove from his wages, then in five years travels in a limousine, in ten years is the founder of a city, is a millionaire or a senator—it's the American Eden."

Despite his sarcasm about his newfound home, he pushed on to Key West in 1924. When friends asked why he chose a remote, rundown village, he said he suffered from "islomania," an obsession with islands. In the decades to come, Key West became a center for writers and artists, but Dos Passos was the first.

Manhattan Transfer became an instant bestseller, and Dos Passos went from struggling unknown to famous writer. His writing style became known as stream of consciousness and was soon copied by other writers. Dos Passos also had a knack for making friends both in the United States and Europe, and soon he was telling anyone willing to listen about the wonders of Key West.

He became a one-man public relations agency for Key West. In the mid-1920s, he reconnected with Ernest Hemingway, and the two became fast friends. At once, he began working on Hemingway, writing to him in 1928, "It's the best place for Ole Hem to dry out his bones."

Hemingway met Dos Passos during World War I, when both were ambulance drivers, the start of a friendship that ended two decades later in Spain. Dos Passos became the more famous of the duo, writing his widely praised *Three Soldiers* while Hemingway sought markets for his writing.

The two exchanged scores of letters, and in many Dos Passos called for a reunion in Key West.

When Dos Passos arrived, he met Katharine Smith, known as Katy. She was passing through Key West from a trip to Mexico when the two met. It seemed as though nothing would come of the meeting—he was finishing his book *The 42nd Parallel* and preparing for a trip to the Soviet Union. They reconnected the following year in Key West and married five months later.

Dos Passos wrote to Edmund Wilson that he was "licking his wounds, fishing, eating wild herons and turtle steak, drinking Spanish wine and Cuban rum and generally remaking the inner man." He told Wilson that Key West was "a swell jumping-off place, the one spot in America desperately unprosperous."

He was right about the island being desperately unprosperous. The Great Depression brought economic ruin, forcing the island into bankruptcy and creating a unique situation where the state government took over its administration. A century after being the richest county in the nation, it was among the poorest.

Until the highway was built, it was difficult to get to the island. The island's problems were endless. The railroad connecting the island with the outside world was heavily damaged in a 1935 hurricane, and there was no effort to rebuild it—parts of it eventually were turned into the 138-mile Overseas Highway, which Ernest Hemingway worried would flood the island with tourists and turn it into another Atlantic City. It made getting to Key West as difficult as it had been in the 1800s.

Dos Passos wrote to a friend, "The railroad has folded and now you arrive by car ferry from a point below Homestead on the mainland. There were three separate ferry rides and sandy roads through the scrubby keys between." Still, his love affair with the island continued, and he called it a "most delightful trip, with long cues of pelicans scrambling up off the water and man o' war birds in the sky and bobby gulls on the buoys and mullet jumping in the milky shallows."

He and Katy purchased a home at 1401 Pine Street, on the edges of the town. He could walk to the downtown area in about fifteen minutes and reach Hemingway's house in about the same time.

ERNEST HEMINGWAY

For Hemingway and his wife, Pauline, the attraction was not Key West or Dos Passos. Rather it was a yellow Ford runabout. Pauline was the niece of Gustav Pfeiffer, who had made his fortune in the patent medicine business (his company began the giant pharmaceutical company Warner-

Ernest Hemingway's routine was to write in the morning and fish in the afternoon. *Florida Archives.*

Lambert). He was known for his generosity, often buying homes for friends and relatives. He wanted to give his niece and her husband a new car and arranged for the dealer in Key West to have it waiting as the couple passed through from Cuba.

The couple arrived, but the car did not. The owners of the Trev-Mor Ford Agency were also the owners of the Trev-Mor Hotel, actually some rooms located above the dealership. They offered to let the couple stay in their hotel until the car arrived.

The delay turned out to be two weeks, enough time for Hemingway to complete *A Farewell to Arms* and to fall in love with Key West. Uncle Gus bought them the largest house on the island. It was built in 1851 by Asa Tift, a shipbuilder and captain who used slave laborers. His descendants had financial troubles, and the house was sold to Uncle Gus for $8,000 in back taxes.

The home was in poor condition, neglected for years, and required major renovations. It was built on the second-highest point on the island—sixteen feet—and was the first to have indoor plumbing, with water supplied by a large cistern on the roof. It was across the street from the lighthouse, and friends claimed that the beam from the lighthouse guided Hemingway home after a night of heavy drinking.

Dos Passos wrote that Hemingway settled in quickly. "He knew all the barkeeps in the little bars. He was cozy with the Spaniards who ran the restaurants. He'd made friends with the family that owned the hardware store where they sold fishing tackle, and he was a conch with the conchs… who handled the commercial fishing boats."

Hemingway called Key West "the St. Tropez of the poor," a backhanded compliment.

He wrote in the morning, before the Florida sun made the house uncomfortable, then went fishing or joined friends at a local bar. When *A Farewell to Arms* was published in early 1929, he became more famous. Dos Passos wrote a review for the *New Masses* and proclaimed the book "the best written book that has seen the light in America for a long day."

The Hemingway home was built in the 1850s and today is a museum. *Florida Archives.*

After writing, Hemingway usually headed for a bar or a boat. He made fast friends with Eddie "Bra" Saunders, a charter boat captain, and Joe "Josie" Russell, the owner of Sloppy Joe's. Russell served liquor during Prohibition, smuggling it in from Cuba. Hemingway was prolific in Key West, producing *Death in the Afternoon*, "The Snows of Kilimanjaro," *The Green Hills of Africa*, *To Have and Have Not* and finally *For Whom The Bell Tolls*. It was not only the amount of work he produced in Key West—critics also believe it was the best work of his career.

He was a slow writer—five hundred words a day was considered a good day—sitting in a chair once used by a Key West cigarmaker and typing at a small typing table.

To Have and Have Not features residents in Key West in prominent roles. The plot involves Harry Morgan, a fishing boat skipper trying to survive in the Great Depression. Facing economic ruin, Morgan turns to smuggling from Cuba. His situation becomes dire, and he turns to murder. The title comes from the book's alternating chapters: the wealthy with their yachts and the poor Key West residents trying to survive.

He looked into the future in the book, writing, "What they're trying to do is starve Conchs out of here so they can burn down the shacks and put up apartments and make this a tourist town. That's what I hear, they're buying up lots, and then after the poor people are starved out and gone somewhere else to starve some more, they're going to come in and make it a beauty spot for tourists."

In 1934, Hemingway purchased a boat named the *Pilar* and took regular fishing trips, often with Dos Passos. In his account of life in Florida, *Under the Tropic*, Dos Passos recalled his fishing trips with Hemingway. "Hem had brought along a couple of bottles of champagne which perched on the ice that kept the mullet fresh in the bait bucket. The rule was that you couldn't have a drink until somebody caught a fish."

On one trip, they saw two large sharks attacking a school of dolphins. Hemingway grabbed a rifle and shot one of the sharks. As he brought the wounded shark on board, he picked up a Colt .22 revolver to finish it off. The shark jerked and struck the pistol, which went off. The bullet struck a piece of brass, splintered, and a fragment struck Hemingway in the leg. A week later, the two were out fishing again.

His strongest writing came in 1935 when a vicious hurricane struck the Florida Keys. Cuban forecasts warned about the approaching storm for days, advice forecasters in the United States ignored. The government workers who should have been preparing for the storm were off for the Labor Day holiday. One of the many Great Depression relief programs involved hiring hundreds of World War I veterans to work on the railroad between Miami and the Keys.

As the storm grew closer, officials began to realize its strength and rushed to put together a rescue plan for the railroad workers in the Keys. A train was sent, but it was too late—the storm blew it off the tracks. The storm killed between 400 and 600 people, including 265 veterans. For Hemingway, it was personal; the workers often came to Key West on weekends and drank with Hemingway at Sloppy Joe's, trading stories about the Great War.

As soon as the storm passed, Hemingway went to the site to offer his help and saw bodies scattered everywhere, some in trees. He had seen death in World War I but was shocked at what he found. Hemingway placed the blame on Roosevelt and wrote a vicious article for the *New Masses* calling the deaths murder and blaming the Roosevelt administration.

> *Why were the men not evacuated on Sunday, or at the latest, Monday morning, when it was known there was a possibility of a hurricane striking the Keys and evacuation was their only possible protection?*
>
> *Who advised against sending the train from Miami to evacuate the veterans until four-thirty o'clock on Monday, so that it was blown off the tracks before it ever reached the lower camps?*
>
> *…You're dead now, brother, but who left you there in the hurricane months on the Keys where a thousand men died before you when they were building the road now washed out? Who left you there? And what's the punishment for manslaughter now?*

The friendship with Dos Passos was a bit awkward, as he was usually in debt to Hemingway. Dos Passos received great reviews and literary recognition but not much money. Even *U.S.A.* did not bring him much money. Hemingway's works made regular appearances on the bestseller lists and brought him wealth. And he was married to a wealthy woman in her own right. In 1932, Hemingway gave Dos Passos $200 to cover a bad check. At times, Hemingway sent money without being asked. "I enclose 100 in case you can use it. If you need more, let me know." When Dos Passos came down with rheumatic fever in 1933, Hemingway sent him $1,000. Dos Passos was never able to repay all of the money.

One problem on a small island was a lack of privacy. Everyone knew what was happening, and as Hemingway's fame grew, people who visited the island wanted to meet the famous man. To help the economy, city officials made his address public to encourage tourists. A city brochure listed 48 things to do in Key West, and visiting the Hemingway home was number 18, behind the ice factory and the county courthouse. The move angered Hemingway, although it was difficult to miss such a large house.

In an article in *Esquire* magazine in 1935, he claimed that he had hired a man who appeared to have leprosy to meet visitors at the gate and scare them away.

On a visit to a bar, the bartender asked him if he wanted to settle his delinquent tab. Hemingway protested that he didn't owe any money, and an investigation found that a Hemingway lookalike was signing bar tabs. Rather than becoming angry, Hemingway hired the man to stand near his house and greet sightseers. An unknown number of people left thinking they had the autograph of the famous writer. Still, the tourists were troubling, and he had a high wall built around the house.

To pursue his hobby of boxing, he erected a ring in the backyard and staged matches. He also refereed bouts at the Blue Heron, a local bar featuring regular fights.

While Hemingway was in Spain covering the civil war, Pauline built a swimming pool—the first in-ground pool on the island—which, according to legend, angered him. There are various versions of the swimming pool story, and the truth may involve parts of all of them. The simple version is that while he was away, Pauline spent $20,000 to build a swimming pool in the backyard. Upon his return, Hemingway supposedly said, "Pauline, you spent all but my last penny, so you might as well have that!" With that, Hemingway threw a penny onto the pool deck, which Pauline preserved in concrete.

The real reason for the swimming pool may have been revenge for Hemingway having an affair with journalist Martha Gellhorn. The two met in 1936 at Hemingway's favorite bar, Sloppy Joe's, and soon began an affair that continued in Spain while both were covering the civil war. Pauline heard about the affair and had Hemingway's beloved boxing ring torn down and replaced with the pool.

Pauline and Hemingway divorced in 1940, and he married Gellhorn—his fourth wife.

The swimming pool story is not the only famous story attached to the Hemingway house. Hemingway is supposed to have kept six-toed cats around the house. According to legend, they were favored by sea captains because with six toes they could more easily capture the rats on ships. His widow, Mary, called the cat story an outright lie and his son Patrick recalled there were peacocks but no cats. Others claim there were cats.

Hemingway's wife built a pool while he was out of the country, removing his beloved boxing ring. *Florida Archives.*

Hemingway had a reputation for throwing away friends, often becoming enemies with those who had helped him in the past. The split between Hemingway and Dos Passos took place far from Key West.

For Dos Passos, the 1930s brought changes in his political views and his friendship with Hemingway. Dos Passos had been a social revolutionary and was friendly to the Soviet Union. He wrote favorably about the violent Industrial Workers of the World and defended the accused killers Sacco and Vanzetti. Slowly, he began to question the actions of Josef Stalin and broke completely during the Spanish Civil War. He went to Spain with his friend Hemingway, but the two grew apart, with Dos Passos questioning what he saw as Hemingway's support for the communist cause.

Once Hemingway split with a friend, his vitriol increased. He wrote an angry letter to Dos Passos recalling the money he had lent him in the past. "When people start in being crooked about money, they usually end up being crooked about everything." Although Hemingway wrote, "Now, I won't send the letter," he did send it and added a paragraph. "So long, Dos,

Hemingway's favorite bar was Sloppy Joe's, where he drank nearly every day and met his future wife. *Florida Archives.*

Hope you're always happy. Imagine you always will be. Must be a dandy life.…Honest Jack Passos'll knife you three times in the back for fifteen cents and sing Giovanezza free."

Of Hemingway, Dos Passos said, "You think for a long time you have a friend, and then you haven't."

World War II took Dos Passos far from Key West, to report on the war in the Pacific and Europe. In 1947, his beloved Katy died in an automobile crash that cost him an eye. Key West became a memory.

After the divorce, Hemingway owned the house, while Pauline lived in it with her two sons until her death in 1951. Hemingway was an infrequent visitor, living primarily in Cuba and Idaho, stopping in Key West as he moved between the two. Hemingway, who suffered from depression, died by suicide at his Idaho home in 1961. The Key West home was sold in 1964 for $80,000 and turned into a museum.

WALLACE STEVENS

Wallace Stevens finally won the Pulitzer Prize for poetry the year he died, a third of a century after he began writing poems. Which Wallace Stevens won the Pulitzer Prize? Was it the strait-laced Hartford attorney who became vice president of one of the nation's largest insurance companies or was it the feuding, fighting, hard-drinking man who escaped to Key West each year?

Stevens was born in 1879 in Pennsylvania, the son of a wealthy lawyer. After graduating from Harvard University, he received his law degree from New York University.

He fell in love with Elsie Moll Kachel, whom his family considered beneath their social position. He married her anyway and never spoke to his father again.

In 1916, he joined Hartford Accident and Indemnity Company, a century-old firm that grew dramatically after weathering disasters such as the Chicago Fire and the San Francisco Earthquake while other firms failed.

By day, he worked on legal matters and at night retreated to a dark corner of his large home and wrote poetry.

He became a vice president, which allowed him to travel more to meetings and conventions. His increased income also enabled travel to Paris and New York, where he found the literary community lacking.

In 1922, he made his first trip to Key West as part of a business trip— becoming one of the first writers in Key West. "This place is paradise— midsummer weather, the sky brilliantly clear and intensely blue, the sea blue and green beyond what you have ever seen."

He usually stayed at the Casa Marina, a luxurious retreat built by Henry Flagler. He was also a regular at the Long Key Fishing Camp, an exclusive resort where he fished with friends. He wrote, "I was christened a charter member of the Long Key Fishing Club of Atlanta. The christening occupied about three days and required just two cases of Scotch. When I traveled home, I was not able to tell whether I was traveling on a sound or a smell. As I remember it, it was very much like a cloud full of Cuban senoritas, coconut palms, and waiters carrying ice water."

One attraction of Key West was that he could use business as an excuse for trips, allowing the Hartford to underwrite most of his expenses. Over the next eighteen years, he spent several weeks a year in Key West and came

Poet Wallace Stevens was one of the few writers who could afford to stay at Key West's Casa Marina. *Florida Archives.*

down for occasional shorter business trips. He wrote to his wife. "This is one of the choicest places I've ever been to. The place is a paradise."

His wife was a passionate homemaker—some said she was obsessed with housekeeping—and remained behind in Hartford. That was fine with Stevens.

The small island began to attract more writers, including two who became his enemies, Ernest Hemingway and Robert Frost.

Stevens met Frost at Casa Marina, and the two became friends. Stevens had been coming to Key West for a dozen years before Frost made his first trip in 1935. Frost was already a well-known poet, with two Pulitzer Prizes. Stevens had published only a single volume of poetry with far less notice.

Although Stevens welcomed Frost with a basket of fruit, that night things went wrong. Stevens was drunk and made comments Frost did not like. Later, in a speech at the University of Miami, Frost talked about Stevens's drinking.

He also feuded with Hemingway. In 1936, the two were in Key West at the same time. "This year he came again pleasant like the cholera," Hemingway wrote.

In Hemingway's version, his sister Ura came home crying because of critical comments Stevens made about Hemingway's writing. Hemingway found Stevens and told the story this way:

> So who should show up but poor old Papa and Mr. Stevens swung that same fabled punch but fortunately missed and I knocked all of him down several times and gave him a good beating. Only trouble was that the first three times I put him down I still had my glasses on....after I took them off Mr. Stevens hit me flush on the jaw with his Sunday punch bam like that. And this is very funny. Broke his hand in two places.

When Stevens returned to Connecticut, he still had a puffy eye and a broken hand.

Hemingway said Stevens tried to make up, but the feud continued. Hemingway wrote, "I don't know anybody needed to be hit worse than Mr. S."

Novelist John Dos Passos also saw Stevens drunk when the poet showed up uninvited at a party in the Dos Passos home. Stevens also managed to offend Marjorie Kinnan Rawlings, the author of *The Yearling*. He visited her Cross Creek home and called her "a very remarkable woman in her own right as distinct from her literary right."

Stevens wrote extensively about Florida, beginning with his first book of poetry, *Harmonium*. One of his poems was "Fabliau of Florida":

Barque of phosphor
On the palmy beach,
More outward into heavy,
Into the alabasters
And night blues.
Foam and cloud are one,
Sultry moon monsters
Are dissolving.
Fill your black hull
With white moonlight,
There will never be an end
To this droning of the surf.

He also wrote an article for the *Atlanta Journal* Sunday magazine about the early cattle kings of Florida with their "saddle bags filled with gold left lying on the front porch or even in the stable. Coffee cans or kitchen pots filled to the brim with the yellow Spanish coins and left unguarded on kitchen shelves of isolated ranch homes!"

His most famous poem is "The Idea of Order in Key West":

She sang beyond the genius of the sea.
The water never formed to mind or voice,
Like a body wholly body, fluttering
Its empty sleeves; and yet its mimic motion
Made constant cry, caused constantly a cry,
That was not ours although we understood.
Inhuman, of the veritable ocean.

He opened his 1936 book, *Ideas of Order*, with the poem "Farewell to Florida," which tells of leaving his paradise in Key West:

Go on, high ship, since now, upon the shore,
The snake has left its skin upon the floor.
Key West sank downward under massive clouds
And silvers and greens spread over the sea. The moon
Is at the mast-head and the past is dead…

He had been one of the Key's first writers, but now they were everywhere in Key West, and while most writers and artists celebrated the island's artistic climate, he wrote, "Key West unfortunately, is becoming rather literary and artistic."

Stevens's visits stopped at the beginning of the American entry into World War II. The government seized his beloved Casa Marina Hotel for military use, and Key West was no longer the secluded getaway he discovered in 1922. It had become a popular resort, which displeased Stevens. "Key West is no longer quite the delightful affection it once was. Who wants to share green cocoanut ice cream with these strange monsters who snooze in the porches of this once forlorn hotel." But there were also the run-ins with other authors, including Hemingway and Frost.

JAMES MERRILL

For James Merrill, the move to Key West was a return to his roots dating back to the 1800s. All of his grandparents were from Florida, and his mother lived in Jacksonville and his father in nearby Green Cove Springs.

James Merrill loved the old Florida his parents and grandparents knew, not the Florida that emerged beginning in the 1920s. "This for me, accordingly, represents the 'real' Florida, as distinguished from the geriatric or economic ghettos proliferating to the south."

His father, Charles Merrill, left Green Cove Springs and founded Merrill Lynch, which became one of the world's leading brokerage firms. James Merrill was born a year after his father married, and he grew up with every advantage, including private schools and Amherst College. He lived in a fifty-room mansion in the Hamptons.

At Amherst, he began writing poetry and published his first book soon after his graduation. He met David Jackson, who became his partner as they moved from Amherst to Connecticut, and in 1978 the two rented a two-room house on Whitehead Street, sharing it with their landlord. The move was David's idea, which Merrill mentions in his poem about moving to Key West, "Clearing the Title":

> *Because the wind has changed, because I guess*
> *My poem (what to call it though) is finished,*
> *Because the golden genie chafes within*
> *His smudged-glass bottle, and, God help us, you*
> *Have chosen, sight unseen, this tropic rendezvous*

Where tourist, outcast, and in-groupie gather
Island by island, linked together,
Causeways bridging the vast shallowness

The poem was published in the *New Yorker* in 1981, the same year Merrill and Jackson purchased a home on Elizabeth Street at the top of Solares Hill, the highest point on the island.

He also wrote "Developers at Crystal River," which deals with the warm waters at Crystal River, which are home to manatees. It reflects Merrill's roots, the Florida that belonged to his parents and their parents. As a child, his parents must have spoken of the manatees gathering at the Green Cove Springs pier to feast on the vegetation.

These are the Springs:
From deep below the bottom of white sand
Mercurial baubles effervesce
To aerate
A glassed-in-bower of bliss
They keep at 74 degrees

"Key West, when I first began to winter there, struck me as preserving a touch or two of that original innocence: great trees, cracked sidewalks, the sociable cemetery. I hope I disappear before they do," Merrill wrote.

For a man who had almost unlimited wealth, the Key West house was modest and required massive renovation to make it livable. The entire house would have fit in the music room of the Hamptons' mansion.

The move and the new house were supposed to be a new beginning for a relationship that was beginning to fray. Jackson gave Merrill a ring, and the two signaled a new commitment.

Jackson and Merrill conducted seances with a Ouija board, publishing the messages from beyond in *The Book of Ephraim.*

Merrill won the Pulitzer Prize for poetry in 1977. His fame grew; in addition to the Pulitzer Prize, there were two National Book Awards and acclaim from critics. Jackson wrote novels that were never published and lived in Merrill's shadow.

As one observer noted, by the time they moved to Key West, they were more roommates than lovers, living on opposite sides of the house.

Alison Laurie watched the relationship disintegrate. She wrote that "it all [began] to go bad, slowly at first and then faster." She said Jackson took "disreputable friends and lovers," and Merrill became involved with the actor Peter Hooten, setting off a competition between Jackson and Hooten for Merrill's attention. As Hooten emerged as the favorite, Jackson drank more. Merrill watched Jackson's decline and said, "He doesn't realize, he doesn't think—he doesn't use his mind anymore. And you know, if you don't, it's like any muscle, it atrophies."

Jackson attracted increasingly disreputable partners for his trysts, often men who were on various drugs and had criminal records. They would use their admission to the home to steal anything from money to clothing. Jackson pretended there were no thefts, while Merrill became more exasperated. He started spending less and less time in Key West and more in a family apartment in New York. Eventually, Merrill abandoned Key West except for brief visits, as the health of both men deteriorated.

Merrill contracted HIV, then AIDS, and died in Arizona while vacationing in 1995.

In her book about the decline of Merrill and Jackson, Laurie writes,

> *Key West has changed too…and not for the better. It was no longer a little-known paradise for writers and artists. There were more tourists, more expensive motels and guesthouses, more T-shirt shops. Huge floating-hotel cruise ships had begun to dock, often blocking the sea view from Mallory Dock for most of the day. The worst thing about it was that those of us who had recently discovered the island were guilty of these changes. Earlier winter residents had been more discreet; they might mention the island in a poem or a story, but they didn't write articles about it for glossy travel magazines and newspapers, as we naively did.*

ELIZABETH BISHOP

Elizabeth Bishop had a comfortable but chaotic childhood, shuttled from relative to relative after the death of her parents. She graduated from Vassar College, then traveled extensively using funds from a family trust and her lover, Louise Crane, the heiress to the Crane Stationery fortune.

She came to Key West in the late 1930s, drawn by the fishing and the colors and lights of the island. She found inspiration for her poems and watercolors. In 1938, she and Crane purchased a home at 624 White Street. She spent a decade there, with Crane and later Marjorie Stevens. In a letter to a friend, she wrote, "It is very well made with slightly arched beams so that it looks either like a ship's cabin or a freight car."

In Key West, she published *North and South—A Cold Spring*, which won the Pulitzer Prize in 1956. Despite the fame that came with the Pulitzer Prize, it brought little money. The first printing was 2,000 copies, a respectable number for a book of poetry, but after she won the Pulitzer, Houghton Mifflin limited the second printing to just 750 copies.

She became friends with Pauline Hemingway, the ex-wife of Ernest, and fit in well with the writing community.

While in Florida, Bishop wrote the poem "Florida." Although it begins with "The state with the prettiest name," it quickly takes a turn to describe a state where

> *the state that floats in brackish water,*
> *held together by mangrove roots*
> *that bear while living oysters in clusters,*
> *and when dead strew white swamps with skeletons*
> *dotted as if bombarded, with green hummocks…*
> *like ancient cannon-balls sprouting grass.*
> *The state full of long S-shaped birds, blue and white,*
> *And unseen hysterical birds who rush up the scale*
> *Every time in a tantrum.*

She also wrote "The Bight," which deals with a coastline that dips inward. She was writing about a bight in Key West. The poem is unusual in that much of it comes from a letter she wrote to the poet Robert Lowell.

> *At low tide like this how sheer the water is.*
> *White, crumbling ribs of marl protrude and glare*
> *and the boats are dry, the pilings dry as matches.*
> *absorbing, rather than being absorbed,*
> *the water is the bight doesn't wet anything,*
> *the color of the gas flame turned as low as possible.*
> *One can smell it turning to gas; if one were Baudelaire*
> *one could probably hear it turning to marimba music.*
> *The little ochre dredge at work off the end of the dock*
> *already plays the dry perfectly off-beat claves.*
> *The birds are outsize. Pelicans crash*
> *into this peculiar gas unnecessarily hard,*
> *it seems to me, like pickaxes,*
> *rarely coming up with anything to show for it,*

and going off with humorous elbowings.
Black-and-white man-of-war birds soar
on impalpable drafts
and open their tails like scissors on the curves
or tense them like wishbones, till they tremble.
The frowsy sponge boats keep coming in
with the obliging air of retrievers,
bristling with jackstraw gaffs and hooks
and decorated with bobbles of sponges…

Behind Bishop's seemingly idyllic life there were demons. She battled alcoholism all of her adult life, probably causing the breakup with Crane and bringing her relationship with Stevens to an end. For Bishop, Key West lost its charm, and she sold the house with the provision that future owners make no structural changes.

Without the house as her anchor, she became a nomad, traveling the world as her funds slowly ran out, until she settled in Brazil, where she lived with Lota de Macedo Soares for sixteen years. When Soares died in 1967, Bishop returned to the United States and began drinking more heavily. She died in 1979, Key West a distant memory.

TENNESSEE WILLIAMS

Tennessee Williams came to Florida in 1939 after graduating from the University of Iowa and worked briefly as a telegraph operator—regular employment always eluded Williams. A few years later, he discovered Key West, seeking to escape after the critics in Boston ravaged his play *Battle of Angels*. The play ran just two weeks before closing while setting off a fury among censors who objected to its sexual nature, particularly one of the women saying her fellow women suffered from "sexual malnutrition."

He thought Key West would be the perfect place to rewrite *Battle of Angels*—offering him a refuge and a chance to swim. "Key West was the southernmost point in America. I figured I'd be able to swim there."

With his limited funds, he found a cabin that had been the slave quarters to a once-grand mansion. He wrote to a friend, "I am occupying the old servant's quarters in back of this 90-year-old house. It has been converted into an attractive living space with a shower. The rent is $7 a week."

If he was seeking quiet to work, he failed to find it. His cabin was "at the center of the action for the pub-crawlers and the night people. Navy officers,

Tennessee Williams stayed in a small cabin during his first visit, but success enabled him to buy a beautiful home. *Florida Archives.*

singers, entertainers, artists, and writers, and some members of the town's social set."

His effort to rewrite the play dragged on, and it took seventeen years before a vastly different version appeared on Broadway. Helped by the fame he had achieved in the intervening years, it managed to run sixty-eight performances. His name was sufficient to have it sold to the movies, starring Marlon Brando and Anna Magnani, although the title was changed to *The Fugitive Kind*. While the play is revived occasionally, it remains his most forgotten work.

When World War II started, Williams took a job with the Corps of Engineers in Jacksonville decoding messages—another failure in his employment history. He later wrote that with "the awful shortage of manpower in those war years, even I impressed the personnel manager as an employable person." He said that he and a coworker—he claimed the man had been prematurely discharged from an asylum—worked overnight, although Williams spent most of his time writing plays.

One night, he overlooked an important message and was fired. "Our boss thought it best to let me go and retain the services of the certified loony."

One of the plays he worked on during the long nights in Jacksonville was *The Glass Menagerie*, which opened on Broadway in 1945 as the war was ending. It was a hit, earning him a Pulitzer Prize and the New York Drama Critics Circle Award. When he returned to Key West, he was famous.

Williams's rise came after Hemingway departed, and he replaced Hemingway as the artistic face of the island. He moved to a cottage, which became the center of the writing community. He could be found at the bar at the Tradewinds with Truman Capote, Carson McCullers, Christopher Isherwood and Gore Vidal. The bar featured a piano, and there was usually singing after a few rounds of drinks.

His income from *The Glass Menagerie* and *A Streetcar Named Desire* allowed him to move from his boardinghouse and purchase a metal-roofed, red-shuttered house on Duncan Street, where he took up painting. He did his greatest work in Key West. In addition to *A Streetcar Named Desire*, he wrote *Summer and Smoke*, *Cat on a Hot Tin Roof*, *Sweet Bird of Youth* and *Night of the Iguana*.

Williams did his part to promote Key West and draw more writers and artists. "This is the most fantastic place that I have been yet in America. It is even more colorful than Frisco, New Orleans, or Santa Fe. There are comparatively few tourists and the town is the real stuff. It still belongs to the natives who are known as 'conks.'"

He wrote *The Rose Tattoo* in Key West, and it ran on Broadway in 1951 for 306 performances. While it was set in Mississippi, Williams insisted the movie version be filmed in Key West. The film was a success, earning three Academy Awards.

While Williams is best known for his plays, he also produced two volumes of his poems, *In the Winter of Cities* in 1956 and *Androgyne, Mon Amour* in 1977. One of the poems in *Androgyne, Mon Amour* is "The Diving Bell," a poem about the divers who go out each day from the docks in Key West:

> *I want to go under the sea in a diving-bell*
> *And return to the surface with ominous wonders to tell.*
> *I want to be able to say:*
> *"The base is unstable, it's probably unable*
> *To weather much weather,*
> *Being all hung together by a couple of blond hairs caught*
> *In a fine-toothed comb."*

Williams found Key West to be forgiving, even welcoming, in regards to his homosexuality, although there was the occasional minister who urged

The Rose Tattoo with Burt Lancaster was set in Mississippi, but Tennessee Williams insisted it be filmed in Key West. *Florida Archives.*

the island to mend what they saw as its evil ways. In 1979, a minister took out an advertisement in the *Key West Citizen*: "If I were chief of police, I would get me a hundred good men, give them each a baseball bat and have them walk down Duval Street and dare one of these freaks to stick his head over the sidewalk. That is the way it was done in Key West in the days I remember and love." The minister told an interviewer what awaited Key West: "We'll either have a revival of our society or the homosexuals will take it over in five years."

The ad appeared amid growing tension over the gay presence in Key West, touching off a series of events: Williams's gardener was found dead in a pool of blood with bullet wounds in his head and neck; a few days later, Williams's home was burglarized; and some of his discarded writing notes were stolen. Finally, Williams and his biographer, Dotson Rader, were leaving a gay disco club called the Monster off Duval Street when they were attacked by four or five young men. Williams was knocked down and Rader punched. Williams held his ground, saying later, "There are punks here."

His presence attracted other gay men, and the Williams cottage became a stopover for many of them.

Williams became a tourist attraction as Hemingway had a generation before. Unlike Hemingway, who could ignore the tourists seeking an autograph or a handshake, Williams reveled in the attention. The result was that as his time in the bars increased, the quality of his plays declined.

Williams entertained a never-ending list of guests, including Carson McCullers; Gore Vidal; Tony Award winner Terrence McNally, known for *Frankie and Johnny at the Clair de Lune*; and Jerry Herman, who produced *Hello Dolly* and *La Cage aux Folles*.

Night of the Iguana in 1961 was his final hit, and his later plays such as *The Red Devil Battery Sign*, *Clothes for a Summer Hotel* and finally, *In Masks Outrageous and Austere*, are forgotten.

By the time Tom McGuane met Williams for dinner in the early 1970s, Williams was in decline. "He was always pretty gaga—I don't know what drugs he was using. He put on *Killing Me Softly* and played it over and over until he basically passed out in his food."

Williams was a magnet for writers, including Truman Capote. "He attracted that sort of coterie of excellent gay writers." "Capote was much more interesting and fun than the others."

As his writing faltered, he traveled more, and hotel rooms became his real home. He died in a New York hotel room in a strange tragedy—inhaling an eyedropper bottle cap and choking.

Williams planned his funeral, asking that one of his favorite poems, Wallace Stevens's "The Idea of Order in Key West," be read. He wanted to be buried at sea near where the poet Hart Crane had jumped overboard and committed suicide. His brother ignored his wishes and had him buried in St. Louis, which Williams called "a city I loathe."

HART CRANE

He came very close. He was close to the island he dreamed about when the end came for Hart Crane. His life held so much promise, but at nearly every turn there was a tragedy.

Crane was the son of a prosperous candy maker in Ohio who was best known for creating Life Savers. Unfortunately for the Crane family, his father was also the man who sold the rights to Life Savers for a few thousand dollars.

Crane's parents fought constantly, and when he was sixteen, he made his first attempt to commit suicide. Crane dropped out of high school and headed for New York, planning to go to college, but ending up as a writer for mail-order catalogues. He moved back to Cleveland, then returned to New York.

His greatest writing came in 1930 at age thirty-one when he produced his classic *The Bridge*. The poem was a nine-part epic anchored by the Brooklyn Bridge. It conveys the power of the city and urban life and was the high point of his career. It brought him some fame but very little money.

He drank heavily and moved from one sexual relationship to another in an age when homosexuality was almost always kept secret. His depression was eased by receiving a Guggenheim Fellowship, allowing him to travel to Mexico to write, although heavy drinking dashed hopes for accomplishing anything.

In Mexico, he created a file folder titled "Key West: An Island Sheaf," with a table of contents and poems in various stages of completion. The fifteenth poem in the file is "Key West," a poem that is almost impossible to understand. He never explained why he wanted to write about Key West. The island had already become known as a writers' haven, although one critic has suggested that he embraced Key West because it was not Ohio.

Crane began his first heterosexual relationship in Mexico, ironically with Peggy Baird, the wife of one of his greatest supporters, Malcolm Cowley. It was Cowley who called *The Bridge* the greatest American poem since Walt Whitman's *Leaves of Grass.*

Baird and Crane booked passage on the USS *Orizaba* to sail from Veracruz, Mexico, to New York with a stop in Havana. The cruise was a disaster, although there is confusion about what happened. Crane allegedly had an affair with a male crew member, which led to a severe beating for Crane. Actress Gertrude Berg was a passenger and remembered that Crane had a black eye "and looked generally battered."

On the morning of April 27, 1932, he passed within a short distance of Key West, the closest he would come to the island, then the ship headed north along the Florida coast. The ship was east of Palm Beach when he tried to leap from the railing but was pulled back by a crew member. He went to his cabin and told Baird, "I'm not going to make it, dear. I'm utterly disgraced."

Berg said Crane returned to the railing, "took off his coat, folded it neatly over the railing—not dropping it on deck—placed both hands on the railing, raised himself on his toes and then…suddenly, he vaulted over the railing and jumped into the sea." Berg and the others rushed to the rail. "Just once I saw Crane swimming strongly, but never again."

TRUMAN CAPOTE

On his first night in Key West, Truman Capote was robbed, losing his wallet with credit cards, $2,000 in cash and an address book. He told the police that he went out of his hotel room, and the thief came in. Others, including Tennessee Williams's friend Dotson Rader, believed he was robbed by a male escort he picked up on the street.

Capote came to Key West to work on his book *Answered Prayers*. The book had a long and strange history. Capote began working on it in 1958, and it was not published—in incomplete form—until after his death nearly thirty years later.

Along the way, he sold excerpts to *Esquire* magazine, and part of the deal called for the magazine's editor, Don Erickson, to fly to Key West to pick up the manuscript. Capote had read that Hemingway insisted that his editor at *Esquire*, Arnold Gingrich, come to Key West to pick up his stories, and Capote saw himself as Hemingway's equal.

Answered Prayers was to be the ultimate tell-all, with Capote revealing confidences he had been told over the decades. Capote, Gore Vidal and Williams first met in 1945 when all were beginning their careers. Vidal and Capote fell out over an argument that led to a libel suit, but the friendship between Williams and Capote remained, although with frequent flareups.

Capote used one of the chapters to write a thinly veiled attack on Williams. The chapter "Unspoiled Monsters" features an unflattering portrait of Mr. Wallace, who is clearly Williams. Williams responded with fury: "This thing Capote has written is shockingly repugnant and thoroughly libelous. Capote's a monster of the first order, a cold blooded murderer at heart. He's a liar and everybody knows he is."

The reaction sent Capote into a tailspin, and he increased his intake of drugs and alcohol. It is unclear whether Capote ever wrote any more after the claims about Williams. Williams did forgive Capote, writing to him in 1978, "Even when I was temporarily outraged by that 'monster' piece in *Esquire* I admired, as I have always, your brilliance and artistry."

Williams had the last word, or perhaps the last drawing is more accurate. Williams drew a work titled *A Child's Garden of Roses*, which shows

Truman Capote came to Key West to write *Answered Prayers*. *Library of Congress.*

Capote as a baby with a gun. Several people on the beach have been shot, and their blood drips on the beach—a reference to Capote as an assassin.

The best Capote story involved a night at a local restaurant. The restaurant was packed with tourists who immediately spotted Capote and his friend, playwright Jimmy Kirkwood, who once said that Key West "is a place for lost people who are a little tilted." Truman spotted one couple staring and predicted, "Watch out! They'll be coming over for autographs!" A woman came over and asked Capote to autograph her menu. He signed, and the woman left, but her husband, apparently drunk and jealous, approached and asked, "Are you Truman Capote?" Capote replied, "I was this morning!"

The man unzipped his pants and pulled out his penis and asked, "Can you put your signature on this?" Capote looked at the man's penis and said, "I don't know about my signature, but I can initial it!"

JAMES LEO HERLIHY

James Leo Herlihy came to Key West in 1957 and found the town a "pretty well-kept secret." He "spent all my time exploring, walking the streets. The place was mysterious, funky, indescribably exotic. It had much of the charm of a foreign country, but you had the post office and the A&P and the phone worked, so life was easy."

When Herlihy arrived, he was an unknown, but that quickly changed. His 1958 play *Blue Denim* opened on Broadway and drew praise from the *New York Times*, which called it "a moving play." It ran for just 166 performances but became a successful movie with Carol Lynley, Brandon deWilde and Macdonald Carey.

The play was controversial, with subjects such as teen abortion and sexuality, although the abortion theme was dropped from the movie.

He drew widespread praise from everyone from Eleanor Roosevelt to Tennessee Williams, who called him the most significant new writer since Carson McCullers.

Williams was biased; Herlihy was his protégé almost from the time Herlihy arrived in Key West. Herlihy recalled that before Williams built a swimming pool, the two of them went swimming off the pier nearly every summer day at twilight. "It was inexpressibly comforting to have the daily company of a kindred spirit; just knowing we were involved in the same sort of lunatic pursuit provided some essential ground that meant everything to me."

James Herlihy, author of *Midnight Cowboy* and a protégé of Tennessee Williams, was an unknown when he arrived in Key West in 1957, but that changed when his play *Blue Denim* opened on Broadway. *Key West Art and Historical Society.*

The two met regularly at County Beach to trade lines from their favorite Wallace Stevens poem, "The Idea of Order at Key West." They grew closer in 1976 when Herlihy's mother was dying of cancer. Herlihy and his mother spent three weeks together in Key West as she slowly died. "Tennessee was in Key West during much of that time, and he was enormously considerate. Sent flowers, messages. Cooked for me. Even showed up at the funeral mass, volunteering to act as pallbearer. I was impressed and moved by it all."

Herlihy's most famous work was *Midnight Cowboy*, which was made into a movie starring Dustin Hoffman. At the end of *Midnight Cowboy*, Joe Buck and Ratso Rizzo are seen on a Greyhound bus heading for sunny Florida. Ratso never makes it. The film won an Academy Award for Best Picture.

Key West is the obvious setting in *All Fall Down*, which is set in "Key Bonita." Herlihy's short stories "A Story that Ends with a Scream," and "Ceremony for the Midget" are set in Key West. "The Day of the Seventh Fire" deals with Key West in the 1930s.

Their social group included Jimmy Kirkwood, the co-writer of *A Chorus Line*; Gore Vidal; and Truman Capote.

In the 1960s, Herlihy became involved in the antiwar movement and was an active participant in the counterculture movement. He purchased a cottage, which became a hangout for hippies. He told a friend, "The Bakers Lane cottage became a kind of 'safe house' for the hippies. I protected a fair number of them from the law, who wanted to drive them out of town, and we had love-ins and weddings in the gardens." He came to believe that "the freaks really did have the establishment on the run, and nothing's been the same since."

Soon Herlihy suffered from the same problems that bothered so many other writers—fame was taking its toll. Just as the tourists plagued Hemingway and Williams, they sought out Herlihy. "I'm trying not to repeat the errors of Key West where I had finally become such a public entity there wasn't much for me to chew on."

He wanted to combine his need for quiet to write and help his counterculture friends. He purchased a farm in Pennsylvania to establish a commune and sold the Bakers Lane home in 1973. The change in locations did not help. He started many projects after leaving Key West, not finishing any. He committed suicide in 1993 at the age of sixty-six.

TOM McGUANE

Tom McGuane, who fished Key West as a boy with his father, returned in the late 1960s not just for the tarpon, but for the written word and lifestyle. "It was an easy place to live—it was inexpensive and there was a tremendous amount of juju, shrimpers, bars, hippies, street people, homeless people, dogs, and chickens. It didn't feel like the U.S. in those days—it was like the tropics and very appealing."

He first lived at 123–25 Ann Street, a block east of the wild and wooly Duval Street, much of it boarded up. Distracted by the atmosphere, he moved to 1011 Von Phister Street. During a pair of divorces and marriages, he sold his house and moved to 416 Elizabeth.

Not all of his time in Key West was productive. "There was so much to do, and the life of your contemporaries was so vivid, and there were the bare feet, and the fishing was great, so it was necessary to develop a rigid little program for writing. But in my journal, there's an entry for 1972 that shows Key West as a completely illiterate winter."

McGuane was born in 1939 in Wyandotte, Michigan, a suburb of Detroit. He spent a semester at the University of Michigan, where his grade point average qualified him only for expulsion. He landed at Olivet College, a small private school. He did a bit better. That summer, he went to Harvard, taking part in the school's open admissions programs, and studying creative writing. He tried again at Michigan, then Olivet, finally Michigan State, where he found success. And from there, he went to Yale School of Drama.

At Michigan State, he met Jim Harrison, who would write *Legends of the Fall*. "Whenever we are around each other, we leave with a new enthusiasm to write."

McGuane's first book was *The Sporting Club*. The sale of the movie rights allowed him to buy a small ranch in Montana and a home in Key West.

The island was a dramatic change. "What the hell is everyone doing here anyway? Why aren't they up north working?" "I associated the island with writers, readers, and writing." In 1971, he published *The Bushwacked Piano*, a rewrite of a book he had written in college. This time he not only found a publisher but also sold the movie rights.

He began working on a book about Key West, the story of fishing guides and competition. *Ninety-Two in the Shade* was published in 1973, to great reviews. It received a front-page review in the *New York Times Book Review*.

McGuane wrote the screenplay for the book, then ended up as the film's director. Robert Altman was supposed to direct it and had already scouted the sites. He and the producer argued, Altman quit and the producer told McGuane, "'You're going to have to direct it,' and I did."

The movie was a disaster. Unsure how to end the movie, McGuane filmed three endings, and it is possible to see all three versions. Like other sensational failures such as *Cleopatra*, the movie is better known for what went on behind the camera than in front of them. He had an affair with Margot Kidder, one of the film's stars, and it ended his marriage. He and Kidder were briefly married.

Jim Harrison accompanied McGuane to a screening of the film and said even McGuane panned the film, standing up at the screening and yelling at the screen.

McGuane changed from the serious, steady worker to someone who noticed the bars and the women for the first time. Booze led to more booze, and drugs led to more drugs. And more women.

He gave up drinking and began staying away from Key West. "It had become kind of a grim place. So it's not Key West's fault necessarily. The party was over by the late seventies. People were dispersing, going elsewhere. It had been a hippie town. It had been a rundown town, turned into an opportunity town for late sixties, early seventies hippies, then it turned into a gay town. A gay town and a hippie town are not the same thing."

JIMMY BUFFETT

Beginning with Hemingway, Key West has had an artist who seems to symbolize the island. It was Hemingway in the 1930s and later Tennessee Williams. Beginning in the 1970s, it was Jimmy Buffett. Buffett started out as a journalist after graduating from the University of Southern Mississippi. He worked as a Nashville reporter for *Billboard* magazine, then turned to street singing in New Orleans and moved to Key West in 1971. He started there as a street singer before landing a job at Logan's Lobster House. Buffett recalled that admission was a dollar, and sitting at the front row "table was Truman Capote, John Malcolm Brinnin, Dotson Rader, and a few other people."

Once his reputation as a musician was secure, Buffett turned to writing and enjoyed the same success. His first two books, *Tales from Margaritaville* and *Where Is Joe Merchant?*, each spent seven months on the *New York Times* fiction bestseller list. In 1998, he wrote *A Pirate Looks at Fifty*, which also became a bestseller on the nonfiction list. He became one of eight authors to have a number-one bestseller on both the fiction and nonfiction bestseller list. The list includes John Steinbeck, William Styron and Dr. Seuss.

Jimmy Buffett became the face of Key West following Ernest Hemingway and Tennessee Williams. *Florida Archives.*

Buffett went on to write two children's books with his daughter Savannah Buffett and another novel, *A Salty Piece of Land*, in 2004. It included a compact disc with the song "A Salty Piece of Land," which also became a bestseller.

Buffett, the street musician in flip-flops, became a conglomerate, opening restaurants and residential communities. He moved nearly two hundred miles up the road to Palm Beach, where there are no street musicians.

DAVID WOLKOWSKY

If modern Key West had a father, it is David Wolkowsky. He was born in Miami and as a teenager saw Key West declared the Poorest City in Florida. In 1962, he inherited some old buildings and empty land in Key West and began his renovations, including the old Sloppy Joe's—now Captain Tony's Saloon—as well as the Mallory Square area.

In 1968, he opened the Pier House resort to guests. The *Miami Herald* called it "the turning point in Key West's transformation from washed-up military outpost to funky tourist attraction."

When Capote came to Key West in 1968 and began searching for a place to stay, he met Wolkowsky, who had completed construction on what became Pier House. Capote asked to see the rooms, and after he inspected them, Wolkowsky invited him for a drink in his forty-five-foot luxury trailer just ten feet from the waterfront.

Capote said he wanted to stay in the trailer, and Wolkowsky agreed. Capote spent two months in the trailer writing *Answered Prayers*, which was published after his death.

Wolkowsky played a major role in reshaping Key West. Most of the early writers came because it was a cheap place that asked little of its residents. Robert Frost came because Miami cost too much. Wallace Stevens could afford to stay in luxury at the Casa Marina, but most, like Tennessee Williams, found tiny cottages—four to five hundred square feet was considered roomy—they could afford.

As the island's fame spread, tourism picked up. Cottages no longer rented for seven dollars a week, and T-shirt shops began to replace some of the iconic Duval Street stores.

And the writers changed too. The drinking and drug culture seemed to be part of the distant past. The huge cruise ships came each day to spend a few hours letting passengers get a glimpse of the past, a drink at Tony's or Sloppy Joe's and a visit to the Hemingway home. Jimmy Buffett the singing

David Wolkowsky played a leading role in the revival of Key West and provided a welcome for writers including Truman Capote. *Florida Archives.*

troubadour was gone, and Jimmy Buffett the entrepreneur had moved to Palm Beach.

A new breed of writers moved in, including Ann Beattie, Judy Blume, Meg Cabot and Annie Dillard.

Beattie was born in Washington, D.C., and in her twenties began attracting national attention with her short stories. Her first novel, *Chilly Scenes of Winter*, was made into a film starring John Heard and Mary Beth Hurt. She was the Edgar Allan Poe Professor of Literature and Creative Writing at the University of Virginia.

She explained her move to Key West in a letter: "For the last couple of years, I've stopped saying that I vacation in Key West and admitted, while my husband and I live in Maine during the summer, we've also started living in Key West during the winter."

Beattie wrote, "People who haven't visited Key West, or those who've only had a brief tourist's experience, usually remember that some writer is associated with Key West, but when the Key Wester says, "Elizabeth Bishop?

James Merrill?' they'll say no, it was that guy that wrote the war book, or some book about fish, a fish that went to war....Right: Hemingway."

Cabot was blunt about her reasons for moving to Key West. After talking to her accountant, "We had to do something to lower our taxes and he gave us a list of states." Florida, which has no income tax or inheritance tax, was the most attractive. She moved in 2001. Her historical romances and the diaries of Princess Mia Thermopolis have enthralled millions. "I feel so creative down here; it's so beautiful." She says neighbors push copies of her books through her mail slot with a request for an autograph for their grandchildren.

Annie Dillard won the 1975 Pulitzer Prize for her novel *Pilgrim at Tinker Creek*, but in Key West, she is better known as Annie Dillard the artist. She has achieved fame for her portraits of great writers when they were young.

Judy Blume began writing in the 1960s, but her breakthrough novel, *Are You There God? It's Me, Margaret*, was a bestseller in the 1970s. Her books are found on the list of all-time bestsellers for children's books, and she has more than eighty million books in print in thirty-two languages.

She and her husband, George Cooper, were married in 1982 in Key West, and the two have become major figures there. Cooper founded the Tropic Cinema on the island, and together they launched the Key West branch of Books and Books, which features the books of the island's classic writers. She had help from an iconic figure in the world of books, Mitchell Kaplan.

Kaplan was born in Miami and worked as an English teacher before opening his bookstore, Books and Books. His empire has grown to six bookstores, which double as South Florida gathering places for authors and their fans.

Despite the success of his bookstores, Kaplan is best known for his role in creating what has become the nation's premier literary event, the Miami Book Fair. It draws more than three hundred authors and tens of thousands of literary lovers each fall.

The event began when Miami-Dade College president Eduardo J. Padron asked Kaplan to put on a book event, originally called "Books by the Bay."

It grew from there.

In Key West, the Key West Literary Seminar emerged as one of the leading retreats for writers in the world. In 1983, David and Lynn Kaufelt launched the seminars. David told people he thought Key West was the nation's premier literary gathering place.

At first, the seminar focused on the literary history of Key West, but it expanded to include nearly every genre, and its combination of lectures, tours, parties and readings have made it among the most competitive literary events in the country.

SARASOTA

MacKINLAY KANTOR

Sarasota was a village with just ten thousand residents when MacKinlay Kantor arrived in 1936. It was known primarily as the home of the Ringling Brothers Circus and the magnificent mansion John Ringling built.

Kantor started a literary movement that brought scores of writers and artists to town and led to creating a weekly group that met each Friday for lunch at the Plaza Spanish Restaurant.

He was born in Iowa in 1904, the son of a father who abandoned the family before Kantor was born and a mother who was a journalist who encouraged her son to write. He began writing crime stories for pulp magazines; his publications included *Real Detective Tales*, *Mystery Stories* and *Detective Fiction Weekly*. In 1928, he published his first novel, *Diversey*. He struggled to find markets for his books until *Long Remember* was published in 1934. It was a story of a pacifist civilian caught up in the Battle of Gettysburg and brought him recognition.

He moved his wife and two sons to Sarasota, leaving four years later for London to report on World War II for various publications, including the *Saturday Evening Post* and *Esquire*. When the war ended, he wrote *Glory for Me*, a novel in blank verse. Producer Samuel Goldwyn purchased the rights but then hired Robert Sherwood to write the script. The experience ended unhappily for Kantor. Although the film was "based on a novel by MacKinlay Kantor," the name was changed to *The Best Years of Our Lives* and

McKinlay Kantor loved to play his guitar. He won the 1956 Pulitzer Prize for *Andersonville. Florida Archives.*

won an Academy Award for Sherwood. His book was a critical and commercial failure, but the movie was a hit.

In one of Hollywood's strangest incidents, Kantor was credited with writing the screenplay for *Gun Crazy*, which has become a well-known film noir. It was based on a short story he wrote in 1940 for the *Saturday Evening Post*. In 1992, it was revealed that Dalton Trumbo was the real screenwriter of the movie. Trumbo, one of the Hollywood Ten, had been blacklisted for refusing to testify before the House Un-American Activities Committee's investigation into communism. Kantor passed the money he was paid for the screenplay on to Trumbo.

While in Germany at the end of the war, Kantor was one of those who entered the Buchenwald concentration camp as it was liberated on April 14, 1945. It led him to do extensive research and the result was the 1955 novel *Andersonville*, a novel about the miserable conditions Union soldiers faced at the Confederate prisoner of war camp. In 1956, *Andersonville* won the Pulitzer Prize.

He returned often to the theme of the Civil War in his thirty novels. In 1960, he wrote an article for *Look* magazine titled "If the South Had Won the Civil War." It was so popular that it was turned into a book.

In 1977 he suffered a heart attack and died, but the literary community he began continues to flourish.

JOHN D. MacDONALD

John D. MacDonald moved to Clearwater in 1949 and two years later moved to Sarasota after asking his friend MacKinley Kantor about the quality of the schools in the town. Macdonald found a "softness of the air, the blue of the water, the dip and cry of the water birds, the broad beaches." From his new home in Siesta Key, he could see water everywhere and watched what he called "the armada of pelicans."

Although he had written well-received books and short stories before the move, it was Florida that shaped his writing and created an entire new genre, the environmentally conscious style of crime novel.

MacDonald was born in Sharon, Pennsylvania, in 1916. After high school, he spent two years at the Wharton School of the University of Pennsylvania before quitting and working menial jobs in New York. The hard work taught him the value of a college degree, and he graduated from Syracuse University. In 1949, he received an MBA from Harvard University, and many of his books involve business deals.

John D. MacDonald combined mystery writing with a passion for preserving Florida's natural beauty. *Florida Archives.*

In 1957, he wrote, *The Executioners*, which became the basis for two movies titled, *Cape Fear*. The 1962 version starred Robert Mitchum as an ex-convict who is determined to destroy the man who sent him to prison for rape, played by Gregory Peck. It was MacKinley Kantor who suggested MacDonald write the book—according to legend, there was a wager involved.

For a decade beginning in 1953, he concentrated on hard-boiled crime thrillers with most set in Florida. His first Travis McGee novel, *The Deep Blue Good-by*, appeared in 1964 and influenced a score of authors, including Randy Wayne White, Dean Koontz, James Hall and Tim Dorsey. McGee lives on a houseboat he won in a poker game in Fort Lauderdale. His job description is finding things people have lost or had stolen. He only works when the bills pile up.

Kantor also played a small role in the McGee series. MacDonald originally named his character Dallas McGee, but Kantor said that with the assassination of President Kennedy in Dallas shortly before the first book was published, it might be best to come up with another name. Kantor suggested "Travis," after a California military base.

A Sarasota artist, Syd Solomon, suggested using a color in each Travis McGee book title, hence *A Purple Place for Dying* or *The Green Ripper*. A painting by Solomon hangs in Travis McGee's houseboat, although in *The Long Silver Rain*, it is splattered with blood. McGee wears a Hägar the Horrible wristwatch, a tribute to MacDonald's friend Dik Browne, who created Hagar. Browne migrated to Sarasota and encouraged other cartoonists to follow him.

MacDonald's 1977 bestseller *Condominium* took place on what was clearly Siesta Key. The fictional builder was a mobster who skimped on materials to build a substandard structure that collapses when a hurricane strikes. Half a century later, a condo collapsed in Miami, and questions were raised about the construction of the structure.

MacDonald's books are of the hard-boiled detective genre with an unusual twist: his intense interest in the Florida environment and those who threaten it. Even before the environmental theme appears in the pages of his books, he was an environmentalist. Mystery writer Tim Dorsey said MacDonald was "Florida's Nostradamus. He was writing about protecting our environment long before we knew it was an issue."

MacDonald lined up against projects to dredge and fill Sarasota Bay to create land for more houses, and he was a campaigner for saving the Everglades. He wrote countless letters to the *Sarasota Herald-Tribune* urging action to protect the environment.

He dedicated his book *A Flash of Green* to those who are "opposed to the uglification of America."

Kurt Vonnegut was a fan, writing, "To diggers a thousand years from now, the works of John D. MacDonald would be a treasure on the order of the tomb of Tutankhamen."

One of those he inspired was Carl Hiaasen, who wrote, "Most readers loved MacDonald's work because he told a rip-roaring yarn. I loved it because he was the first modern writer to nail Florida dead-center, to capture all its languid sleaze, racy sense of promise, and breath-grabbing beauty."

Bestselling author Craig Pittman recalled being introduced to MacDonald's work. "I didn't realize that the places I'd enjoyed visiting might someday be turned into cul-de-sacs and convenience stores, or that such changes might not be for the best."

As Pittman pointed out, MacDonald's 1962 book *A Flash of Green* featured a crooked politician who was proposing a ruinous dredge-and-fill project. The book was based on a dredge-and-fill project near his Siesta Key home, despite MacDonald's efforts to stop it. The same year, Rachel Carson published her groundbreaking work *Silent Spring*, which deals with threats to the environment. The two were working to save the economy in entirely different genres.

Historian Jack Davis, who won a Pulitzer Prize for his history of the Gulf of Mexico, wrote, "Having made the state his home, MacDonald sensed personal loss when…business and government leaders impaired the quality of life. Despite his efforts, by 1979, MacDonald said the smell of sweet orange blossoms was fading and the state was 'smelling like a robot's armpit.'"

Stephen King wrote, "John D. MacDonald has written a novel called *The End of the Night* which I would argue is one of the great American novels of the twentieth century. It ranks with *Death of a Salesman*, it ranks with *An American Tragedy*."

MacDonald was a charter member of the Liars Club, which met every Friday at the Plaza Spanish Restaurant on First Street. It drew a prestigious list of writers and artists. Today, it continues in another location.

The importance of Siesta Key became clear when MacDonald underwent open-heart surgery in Milwaukee. There were surgical complications, and as MacDonald slipped into a coma, he spoke his final word, "home."

TERRENCE McNALLY

Terrence McNally was born in 1938 in St. Petersburg, where his parents operated a bar and grill on the beach. The family moved several times, but along the way, McNally acquired a love for Broadway shows. He remembered his first musical, *Annie Get Your Gun*, in 1946 with Ethel Merman. After graduating from Columbia University, he secured a job as a tutor for John Steinbeck's two sons on a family trip around the world. He finished a draft of *And Things That Go Bump in the Night*, which was a flop, but it was also the first play to feature the theme of homosexuality. He went on to win five Tony Awards for plays, including awards for *Frankie and Johnny in the Clair de Lune*, *Kiss of the Spider Woman*, *The Full Monty* and *Ragtime*. McNally brought property in 1997 with his then-partner Murphy Davis. They bought identical side-by-side cottages. When they broke up, the property was sold.

McNally and his husband, Tom Kirdahy, purchased a condo in Sarasota in 2017. "We had a place in Key West, but it became increasingly clear that Terrence could no longer do the stairs. We needed a place where he could be in the sun, but also a place that could be very private for us, where we would not run into people we know every day."

McNally became an alcoholic, but he got sober in the 1980s. He recovered from lung cancer, which left him with severe breathing problems requiring him to use oxygen. In his weakened condition, he fell victim to COVID and died in Sarasota Memorial Hospital.

JOHN JAKES

John Jakes moved to Sarasota from Hilton Head Island. "This area has always been a magnet for writers. I can't exactly tell you why, but it has been."

John Jakes became involved with supporting cultural affairs after moving to Sarasota. *Courtesy Selby Memorial Library.*

After twenty-two years of writing, he became a sensation with *The Kent Family Chronicles* and followed it with *North and South*.

"I knew of Sarasota a long time ago," said Jakes, who became a snowbird here with his wife of fifty-five years, Rachel, in 2003. "I knew of Sarasota a long time ago because of the mystical attraction it seemed to have for writers, namely the most revered John D. MacDonald and my friend, Evan Hunter [creator of Ed McBain]. I knew about the Liars Club and then Stuart Kaminsky started working on me to move down." Another draw was the cultural life in Sarasota. He attended Rotary Club meetings and Cincinnati Reds games.

Like other authors who moved to Florida, he set a routine for writing. "I work every day, five days a week from about 8:30 in the morning to 2:00 in the afternoon."

STUART KAMINSKY

Stuart Kaminsky was one of those authors who found inspiration and friendship in the Sarasota writer's colony. He was born in Chicago and attended the University of Illinois, where he majored in journalism and received a doctorate in film studies from Northwestern University.

He spent a quarter-century teaching before turning to writing full time, creating a series of Hollywood-themed books. He turned out two or more books a year, producing more than sixty crime novels.

His first novel appeared in 1977, *Bullet for a Star*, which introduced Toby Peters, a 1930s private eye in Hollywood. Kaminsky's sons were named Toby and Peter. Peters is called on to save Errol Flynn from a blackmailer. Other books include Judy Garland as a client to figure out who murdered a Munchkin and helping Cary Grant solve a mystery. He also created other characters, including Abe Lieberman, a Chicago cop; Lew Fonesca, a process server in Sarasota; and Moscow detective Porfiry Rostnikov.

He earned a 1989 Edgar Award for best novel and in 2006 was named a Grand Master by the Mystery Writers of America—the organization's highest award. His work inspired other writers, including Sara Paretsky, who dedicated her first V.I. Warshawski private-eye book to Kaminsky.

He died from hepatitis C, which he contracted as an army medic in the 1950s.

STEPHEN KING

Stephen King has been a supporter of Sarasota's Selby Memorial Library. *Courtesy Selby Memorial Library.*

Stephen King was already world-famous when he purchased an $8.9 million home on Casey Key in 2001. At the time, it was the most expensive home ever purchased in Sarasota County.

He first came to Sarasota in 1999 when he rented a condominium on Longboat Key, off Sarasota. King's Maine home on West Broadway in Bangor was already well known—a Victorian mansion with a bronze vampire and bats on its gates.

King was influenced by other Florida writers Elmore Leonard and John D. MacDonald. King sold his first short story in 1967 to *Startling Mystery Stories*, "The Glass Floor." In 1974, *Carrie* was published by Doubleday, sending him up the bestseller list.

MacDonald has served as an inspiration to King in more than literature. King has become involved in political movements and became a frequent critic of Republic governors Rick Scott and Ron DeSantis. He participated in a demonstration for women's rights and is a strong supporter of protecting the environment.

He has also been a supporter of Sarasota bookstores and the city's Selby Public Library. King is a frequent visitor at Bookstore 1 Sarasota, a private bookstore. He once showed up for a book signing and brought his friend John Grisham. The Selby Library has been a major beneficiary of the presence of King and other writers, who are frequent speakers.

CRUSADERS FOR JUSTICE

ALBERY A. WHITMAN

Albery A. Whitman is all but forgotten today, but for a time in the 1800s, he was ranked with Paul Dunbar as one of the greatest African American poets.

Whitman was born into slavery in 1851, and his parents died when he was twelve years old. Unable to read or write, he moved north at the end of the Civil War and attended Wilberforce University.

He began writing poetry in college and published his first book, *Leelah Misled*, in 1873. In 1884, he wrote *The Rape of Florida*, later renamed *Twasinta's Seminoles*.

The Rape of Florida tells the story of a romance between Atlassa, a Seminole chief, and Ewald, the daughter of a Maroon woman and a Spanish landowner. It follows the events of the first and second Seminole Wars as the Seminoles and their Maroon allies fight efforts by the United States to drive them from Florida to the West.

Like all his poems, *Rape in Florida* wanders at times, a mixture of commentary, editorializing and memoir.

The Indians are lured by a flag of truce, but it is a trick, and they end up in chains and are sent to Santa Rosa, Mexico.

Whitman died in 1901 at the age of fifty, and while Dunbar's fame increased, Whitman's faded. His daughters, vaudeville stars known as the Whitman Sisters, were better known.

JOHN GREENLEAF WHITTIER

Before Harriett Beecher Stowe stirred the conscience of the nation with *Uncle Tom's Cabin*, John Greenleaf Whittier wrote a poem that evoked the horrors of slavery and the justice system that protected it to the North.

Beginning in 1845, antislavery forces circulated the poem through scores of publications and thousands of handbills, often with "Read and Circulate" at the top to encourage even wider circulation.

Whittier's poem tells the dramatic story of Captain Jonathan Walker, who arrived in Pensacola in 1837. His neighbors were disturbed because Walker treated African Americans with respect—both slaves and free. The upper coast of the Gulf of Mexico had become a prime spot for the illegal importation of slaves—outlawed by the Constitution in 1808.

Slaves were brought into the Panhandle and then moved to plantations throughout the South. Walker worked with seven slaves who begged him to help them flee to the Bahamas and freedom. He loaded them in a small boat and set sail through the gulf. Alarms were soon sounded and a search began.

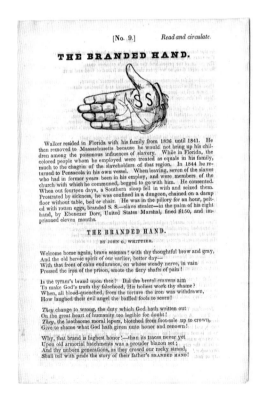

Left: John Greenleaf Whittier's poem about Walker's penalty was widely distributed throughout the nation. *Library of Congress.*

Opposite: The trial of Jonathan Walker shocked the nation the nation and helped mobilize antislavery forces. *Library of Congress.*

United States Marshal branding the author

Walker had underestimated the length of the journey, and after two weeks, they were still at sea and Walker was suffering from sunstroke.

Two sloops captured them and took them to Key West, where he was charged in federal court with aiding the escape of slaves. The slaves were returned to their masters.

A federal jury convicted Walker, fined him $150 and added a bizarre penalty that created an uproar in the North. The federal judge ordered Walker to be branded with the initials "SS" for slave stealer. A brand had to be made to carry out the sentence.

Walker was placed in stocks and pelted with fruit and eggs for an hour, then taken to the courtroom, where a small fire was set to heat the brand. The sheriff carried out the sentence, holding the brand on Walker's palm for fifteen to twenty seconds. He returned to the North, where he was hailed as a hero.

Whittier had been involved in the abolitionist movement for several years and wrote an antislavery pamphlet published by William Lloyd Garrison.

In 1845, he wrote "The Branded Hand."

> *Welcome home again, brave seaman! With thy thoughtful brow and gray,*
> *And the old heroic spirit of our earlier, better day,*
> *With that front of calm endurance, on whose steady nerve in vain*
> *Pressed the iron of the prison, smote the fiery shafts of pain...*
> *Why, that brand is highest honor! than its traces never yet*

Upon old armorial hatchments was a pounder blazon set;
And thy unborn generations, as they treat our rocky strand,
Shall tell with pride the story of their father's branded hand!

HARRIET BEECHER STOWE

Harriet Beecher Stowe became famous and wealthy with her book *Uncle Tom's Cabin.* Her book stirred antislavery forces with its portrait of the treatment of slaves. Some credit her book as a cause of the Civil War.

After the Civil War, she purchased a plantation near Jacksonville as part of a plan to rehabilitate her worthless son, Frederick, and help former slaves.

My plan of going to Florida, as it lies in my mind, is not in any sense a mere worldly enterprise. I have for many years had a longing to be more immediately doing Christ's work on earth. My heart is with that poor people whose cause in words I have tried to plead, and who now ignorant and docile, are just in that formative stage in which whoever seizes has them.

She purchased an old cotton plantation known as Laurel Grove on the St. Johns River near Jacksonville. She made a fortune from her book but found a constant stream of ways to squander it. Her plan called for Frederick to give up drinking and take up cotton planting. The former slaves would work the farm. From the beginning, the plan failed; Frederick was often in Jacksonville drinking, and the crops went to ruin.

Frederick fled the plantation and sailed for California, where he vanished.

Stowe had remained in New York, and when she came to Jacksonville during the winter of 1866–67, she realized the extent of her son's failures. She was not ready to give up on Florida. "We are now thinking seriously of a place in Mandarin much more beautiful than any other in the vicinity." The property had fruit trees on thirty acres.

She built a school for the former slaves, which doubled as a community center and church. She instantly became the state's most famous resident and the state's favorite tourist attraction. The steamboats taking tourists along the St. Johns pointed out her home, and she began coming down to the docks when the ships passed.

Guidebooks such as *Appleton's Illustrated Handbook of American Winter Resorts* and *Florida: Its Scenery, Climate, and History, etc.* included her house. In a single year, fourteen thousand visitors sailed past her home.

Above: Harriett Beecher Stowe's home featured a long dock for steamships to dock to see the great lady. *Florida Archives.*

Left: Stowe wrote columns extolling the wonders of Florida, which drew residents and tourists. *Florida Archives.*

Harriett Beecher Stowe sat with her friends outside her Mandarin home to watch the steamboats go by. *Florida Archives.*

Stowe wrote a series of letters to magazines discussing her life in Florida and offering tips for buying land. A collection of the letters was published in a book, *Palmetto Leaves*, which became a bestseller.

The letters and the book brought more tourists, and she turned her home into an attraction with a 556-foot pier where four steamboats could dock at a time. Her visits stopped in 1884, and the steamboats stopped coming. She died in 1896.

JAMES WELDON JOHNSON

When a hurricane hit the Bahamas in 1866, James Johnson lost his sponge business. He saw no chance of recovering his livelihood and left for Jacksonville and a job as a waiter at the St. James Hotel, the grandest in the city. He was soon promoted to head waiter, a significant job for an African American in the Jim Crow South.

The St. James was the state's first hotel with electricity and a gathering place for wealthy northerners who came each winter.

Five years later, James Weldon Johnson was born. Not only did his father have a steady income, but his mother also was a teacher, who taught him at home before enrolling him at the city's premier all-Black school, Stanton School. He attended Atlanta University and returned to Jacksonville as principal of the Stanton School—he was just twenty-three years old.

The following year, he launched the *Daily American* newspaper, devoted to the African American community. He struggled, trying to put out a daily newspaper in a town of twenty-five thousand people that could barely support a newspaper that came out twice a week.

James Weldon Johnson wrote what has become known as the Negro National Anthem while serving as principal at Stanton School in Jacksonville. *Florida Archives.*

Within a year, it collapsed, Johnson's first failure, "my first taste of defeat in public life." While the paper collapsed, it helped Johnson establish a national reputation. Booker T. Washington and W.E.B. DuBois both became aware of Johnson through his newspaper.

He studied law with a white attorney, in what must have seemed a hopeless endeavor—no African American had been admitted to the Florida Bar since the end of Reconstruction. To the surprise of many, he was admitted to the Florida Bar and built a successful practice while serving as principal at Stanton.

Two events in 1901 convinced Johnson to leave Jacksonville. A massive fire destroyed much of the city. It was particularly devastating in the African American section, which lacked fire protection. He saw his school go up in flames.

The second event was more troubling. A light-skinned African American woman came to town to report on the fire and met Johnson in a nearby park. Word quickly spread that Johnson was seen talking with a white woman, and a white mob with bloodhounds attacked the two. The mob dragged him to police headquarters. He received an apology but realized that even one of the city's leading African Americans was at the mercy of the mob.

He fled to New York, where he and his brother turned their skills to writing music. His timing brought him to the city in the Harlem Renaissance, when the city was alive with African American authors, singers, actors, poets and musicians. Johnson was a star, writing music, literature, and poetry.

President Theodore Roosevelt named him consul to Venezuela and later Nicaragua, where he completed his only novel, *The Autobiography of an Ex-Colored Man.*

In 1916, he was named field secretary of the National Association for the Advancement of Colored People and increased NAACP membership tenfold, to ninety thousand. With this success came promotion to lead the organization—the first Black man to become the executive secretary. He served as the leader for a decade. The increase in membership and branches was not enough to please the NAACP board, which wanted more success with legislation. He stepped down in 1930 to teach at Fisk University.

Johnson is best known for a poem he wrote at the Stanton School in 1900. The school planned a big celebration to mark Abraham Lincoln's birthday, and Booker T. Washington agreed to speak. Johnson wanted to do something special and wrote a poem titled "Lift Every Voice and Sing" for the five hundred students to recite.

Five years later, he and his brother put music to the poem, and in 1919, the NAACP named it "The Negro National Anthem."

The song became a staple at gatherings of African Americans, pasted into the back of church hymnals and recorded scores of times, including versions by Dionne Warwick and Stevie Wonder.

Lift every voice and sing
Till earth and heaven ring
Ring with the harmonies of Liberty
Let our rejoicing rise
High as the listening skies
Let it resound loud as the rolling sea
Sing a song full of the faith that the dark past has taught us
Sing a song full of the hope that the present has brought us
Facing the rising sun of our new day begun
Let us march on till victory is won
Stony the road we trod
Bitter the chastening rod
Felt in the days when hope unborn had died
Yet with a steady beat
Have not our weary feet
Come to the place for which our fathers sighed?

We have come over a way that with tears has been watered
We have come, treading our path through the blood of the slaughtered
Out from the gloomy past
Till now we stand at last
Where the white gleam of our bright star is cast
God of our weary years
God of our silent tears
Thou who has brought us thus far on the way
Thou who has by Thy might led us into the light
Keep us forever in the path, we pray
Lest our feet stray from the places, our God, where we met Thee
Lest our hearts drunk with the wine of the world, we forget Thee
Shadowed beneath Thy hand
May we forever stand
True to our God
True to our native land
Our native land

At the 2009 inauguration for President Barack Obama, the former president of the Southern Christian Leadership Conference, Joseph Lowery, read part of the poem during the benediction.

Johnson died in an automobile crash in 1938.

ZORA NEALE HURSTON

Zora Neale Hurston always returned to Florida. No matter how famous she became, it was her home and her sanctuary. And in the end, it was where she died alone and forgotten.

"I've got a map of Florida on my tongue," she once said.

She was a child when her family moved from Alabama to Eatonville, Florida, a small community on the outskirts of Orlando. It was one of the towns founded by the formerly enslaved and one of the few to survive.

Her mother died when she was young, and her father took her out of school when she was thirteen to care for her siblings. A job as a maid for a white family rescued her from a life of deprivation. Her employer gave her a book—her first—and arranged for her to go to high school and attend Howard University, where she was one of the founders of the school newspaper.

In her junior year at Howard, she transferred to Barnard College, becoming the school's only African American student. Her long journey finally brought her a degree in anthropology and graduate study at Columbia University.

Her time in New York coincided with the Harlem Renaissance as the growing African American community in New York exploded with music, literature and art. Her short story "Spunk" appeared in *The New Negro*, an anthology by African Americans.

In 1929, she moved to Eau Gallie, Florida, a coastal community about an hour's drive from Eatonville. She rented a small cottage and went to work on her book *Mules and Men*, which was finally published to wide acclaim in 1935. She also worked at Bethune-Cookman College, creating the school's drama classes. She wrote more short stories and tried unsuccessfully to collaborate on a play with Langston Hughes.

In 1937, she won a Guggenheim Fellowship to study in Jamaica and Haiti, leading to her first novel, *Their Eyes Were Watching God*.

The book tells the story of Janie and Teacake, who wind up in Belle Glade, Florida. "To Janie's strange eyes, everything in the Everglades was big and new. Big Lake Okechobee [*sic*], big beans, big cane, big weeds, big everything….Ground so rich that everything went wild….People wild too." They arrive as the deadly 1928 hurricane strikes. The storm flooded the area around Lake Okeechobee, and nearly two thousand people died. "It [the wind] woke up old Okechobee [*sic*] and the monster began to roll in his bed. Began to roll and complain like a peevish world on a grumble."

During the Great Depression, Hurston worked for the Works Progress Administration, touring Florida to contribute to a guidebook about the state and conducting interviews with former slaves.

Her fame grew, and she wrote for magazines, including the *Saturday Evening Post*. The realistic portrayals that drew praise in the 1930s led to criticism beginning in the 1940s. She was attacked for her portrayal of Black people, particularly their speech patterns.

Amid the criticism, her personal life was also faltering. There were a couple of

Zora Neale Hurston died broke and forgotten in Fort Pierce. *Florida Archives.*

Author Alice Walker rescued Zora Neale Hurston from obscurity, reintroduced her work to readers and purchased a headstone for her unmarked grave. As a result of her work, the Zora Neale Hurston Festival began. *Florida Archives.*

marriages, one lasting a few years, the other a few months. In 1948, a mother accused Hurston of molesting her developmentally disabled ten-year-old son in New York.

Although such cases involving juveniles are sealed, court employees leaked the information to African American newspapers, which were quick to publish the information. The *Afro-American* ran the story without even contacting Hurston and slanted the story to make Hurston look guilty, even though she was in Honduras when the alleged incident took place.

The mother may have played a role in encouraging the charges and in time the boy admitted he made up the charges. The damage was done, and she never recovered.

By the late 1950s, Hurston was forgotten, with most of her books out of print. She went through job after job, always scratching for money. In 1956, she was hired as a librarian at Patrick Air Force Base in Cocoa Beach but was fired when her white supervisor said she was "too well-educated for the job."

A job teaching at Lincoln Academy in Fort Pierce ended badly, and she found work as a maid. When a national magazine wrote an article about her working as a maid, she was fired by the family, which did not like the publicity.

In 1958, she suffered a series of strokes and was admitted to the St. Lucie County Welfare Home, where she died in 1960. A friend saved her manuscripts from destruction after she died.

She died alone, and it was fifteen years before her reputation was revived. In 1975, Alice Walker wrote a magazine article praising Hurston's writing, which led to a revival of her work. Walker, who would win a Pulitzer Prize for her 1982 book *The Color Purple* also paid to have a tombstone placed on Hurston's unmarked grave site.

MARJORY STONEMAN DOUGLAS

Marjory Stoneman Douglas watched Florida grow, documenting the damage done to her beloved Everglades. *Florida Archives.*

Marjory Stoneman Douglas first came to Florida in 1894 when she was four years old. A century later, she was one of the most famous Floridians. She recalled that she and her parents stayed at the Tampa Bay Hotel, which had opened just three years earlier, and she remembered picking an orange from a nearby tree. Her parents stopped there on their way to Havana. They could not have stopped in Miami—its creation was still two years away.

She grew up in Massachusetts in what could kindly be called a dysfunctional family. Her father went through a series of failed careers while her mother was in and out of mental institutions. After graduating from Wellesley, she married a con man thirty years older, who may have already been married. She escaped by moving to Miami, where her father had founded the *Miami Herald*. The town had about fifteen thousand residents.

She took a job as a society writer in a town with almost no society. She confessed that she fabricated stories to fill her column, creating fictional, high-society characters.

After serving in the navy during World War I, she returned to the *Herald* as a columnist. She began a crusade against convict labor, a cruel system whereby prisoners were leased to private companies and subjected to cruel treatment. One of those who was imprisoned was a young hitchhiker from North Dakota who was beaten to death in a labor camp.

She wrote a poem about the young man, whose death moved the state legislature to eventually outlaw convict leasing:

> *A wind creeps up and it's him it follows.*
> *Martin Tabert of North Dakota is walking Florida now.*
> *They took him out to the convict camp, and he's walking Florida now.*
> *O children, the tall pines stood and heard him when he was*
> *   Moaning low.*
> *The other convicts, they stood around him,*
> *When the length of the black strap cracked and found him.*

Martin Tabert of North Dakota. And he's walking Florida now.
They nailed his coffin boards together and he's walking Florida now.
O children, the dark night saw where they buried him,
*   buried him low.*
And the tall pines heard where they went to hide him.
And the wind crept up to moan beside him.
Martin Tabert of North Dakota. And he's walking Florida now.
The whip is still in the convict camps, for Florida's stirring now.
Children, from Key West to Pensacola you can hear the great wind go.
The wind that he roused when he lay dying,
The angry voice of Florida crying.
Martin Tabert of North Dakota,
Martin Tabert of North Dakota,
Martin Tabert of North Dakota,
You can rest from your walking now.

Douglas left the newspaper in 1923 to do freelance writing, primarily for the *Saturday Evening Post*, which published forty of her stories. In the 1930s, she wrote a pamphlet urging the creation of a botanical garden, her introduction to the environmental movement.

As Florida grew around her simple house and her fame increased, Marjory Stoneman Douglas stayed in her small home. *Florida Archives.*

She became involved with the Everglades through her father, whose newspaper was in a fight with the governor, who wanted to drain the glades. She joined the battle to have the Everglades named a national park, which led to an offer to write a book about the Miami River for the classic Rivers of America Series. She told the editors that she thought the Miami River unworthy of the series and suggested a book on the Everglades, which she called a "River of Grass."

"There, on a writer's whim and an editor's decision, I was hooked with the idea that would consume me for the rest of my life."

Developers wanted to drain the Everglades and build homes and shopping centers. The sugar industry wanted to use it as a dumping ground for waste. And the Army Corps of Engineers was always proposing to build canals or launch its own drainage projects.

In 1947, President Harry Truman dedicated the Everglades as a national park as Douglas's book, *The Everglades: River of Grass* appeared in bookstores. It became a classic, and she followed it with more books.

After her victory in the Everglades, she continued to work for the environment for half a century until her death at the age of 108. When she first came to Florida there were just 400,000 people scattered throughout the state. When she died, there were 15,000,000.

FORGOTTEN BESTSELLERS

REX BEACH

Rex Beach was one of America's bestselling authors; books were turned into plays and movies, but today his works are largely forgotten. He moved to Tampa as a child and had to overcome abject poverty. In his biography, *Personal Exposures*, he wrote, "We Beaches began Florida life in a tent—another fascinating experience for a boy and one which lacked only a visit from a raiding Seminole war party to make it perfect. Then we moved into an unpainted three-room house ventilated with cracks."

The family overcame difficulties, and there was enough money to send Beach to Rollins College, which had a high school at the time. "I went there because for the same reason I ate bananas—it was cheap and I was told it would give me all I needed."

Beach and Rollins did not get along; he seemed to spend much of his time violating school rules, and by his junior year he was facing expulsion. Instead, he quit and headed to Chicago to attend law school.

As he studied law, he read stories of gold discoveries in Alaska and could not resist the urge to join the hordes heading north. After a year, he dropped out and went to seek his fortune. He struck gold, enough to finance his education, and for several years he moved back and forth between mining and law school.

He competed in the 1904 Olympics, finishing second with the Chicago Athletic Association water polo team. Only Americans competed in the event, and the gold medal went to the New York Athletic Club.

He finished law school but decided that neither law nor mining was for him. "I began to suspect that I lacked not only what it took to be a lawyer, but also what is required to make a miner."

He turned to writing, producing thirty-three books, two plays and hundreds of successful stories. He first wrote about his search for gold for *McClure's Magazine*. His second book, *The Spoilers*, was his most successful, selling 700,000 copies. Like much of his writing, it was based on real incidents—in this case the corrupt Alaska officials who stole mines from prospectors. It also became a motion picture—five times. The first was a silent film, and it went on to be filmed four more times. The 1942 version stars John Wayne and Marlene Dietrich, and the 1955 version features Jeff Chandler and Anne Baxter. *The Auction Block* was filmed twice, both times as silent movies.

Rex Beach gave up gold mining and a law practice to turn out a series of bestselling books. *Courtesy Rollins College.*

He became known as the "Victor Hugo of the North," but critics found his work predictable and formulaic. One critic wrote that his work is "mercifully forgotten today."

His sales were declining, and the critics were correct about the predictability.

Beach's financial success enabled him to buy seven thousand acres near Sebring and five thousand acres near Indiantown, where he grew celery and flowers. Using scientific methods, he produced gladiolus bulbs and made a second fortune. His novel *Wild Pastures* is set in the cattle land of southwest Florida. By the 1940s, his health was fragile, and the death of his wife in 1947 accelerated his decline. He developed throat cancer and needed a breathing tube for air and a second tube in his stomach for nourishment.

On December 7, 1949, he killed himself with a gun.

THEODORE PRATT

Theodore Pratt is one of the forgotten Florida bestselling authors. In his time, his books routinely climbed the list of bestsellers and were turned into movies. Pratt and his wife moved to Majorca, where he managed to offend officials with an article, and they were soon back in the United States. They settled in Lake Worth in 1934, and over the next thirty-five years he produced fourteen novels set in Florida.

Theodore Pratt's best-known work is *The Barefoot Mailman*, which was a popular book and a movie based on a true story. Murals based on the book are in the West Palm Beach Post Office. *Florida Archives.*

His work became known for his deep research and detailed knowledge. His novel *The Barefoot Mailman* was published in 1943 and based on the true story of the nineteenth-century mailmen who delivered the mail along Florida's east coast. There were no roads and no guarantee of fresh water, so mail was carried by boat from St. Augustine to Jupiter, with part of the distance covered on foot along the shore. In 1951, it was made into a movie starring Robert Cummings.

He wrote "Land of the Jook," a searing look at life among Florida's migrant workers. The jooks were the clubs where the migrants gathered to drink and dance. "Many of the migrants, white and black continue to live in indescribable squalor in ramshackle camps, boardinghouses, tin and burlap shacks, broken-down trailers, trucks, old automobiles—and the screaming jooks."

Although the jook joints were gathering spots for African American migrant workers, the movie based on the book starred Ronald Reagan and Ann Sheridan. It was called *Juke Girl* and led the term to be gradually changed from "jook" to "juke." His book was so accurate that friends advised him not to venture into the migrant camps around Lake Okeechobee.

In his collection of short stories, *Florida Roundabout*, Pratt offers a penetrating look at aspects of Florida life. He visited a cockfight, medicine show and Holy Roller meeting. He spent months in the Florida Keys writing about people stranded on an island before writing *Mercy Island*, which became a movie in 1941.

Living on the east coast of Florida during World War II, Pratt saw the oil tankers sail by and read about German submarines offshore sinking the tankers. And so, after a life spent writing fact-based stories, he wrote *The Incredible Mr. Limpet*, about a man who turns into a fish to help the navy fight the Nazis. Two decades later, it was made into a movie starring Don Knotts.

Pratt died in Delray Beach in 1969.

ERSKINE CALDWELL

Erskine Caldwell came to Florida as the son of an itinerant preacher, whose church work took him to half a dozen states before Caldwell was fifteen. At the University of Virginia, he began writing short stories for small magazines paying little or nothing.

His work drew the attention of F. Scott Fitzgerald, who recommended him to Max Perkins, the nation's most respected editor.

Caldwell's father's work took him to some of the poorest areas of the South, and he saw the sharecropper shacks and the poverty of the people who lived in them. The Great Depression made conditions even worse.

In 1932, he wrote his wrenching examination of poverty in the South, *Tobacco Road*. It became a bestseller and was widely praised. Saul Bellow thought Caldwell should have won the Pulitzer Prize, and others placed it on lists of best novels.

It became a Broadway play, which ran for eight years, then a movie, which made dramatic changes to make it more acceptable.

He followed it with *God's Little Acre*, dealing with a farmer who searches for gold on his farm while his crops are neglected. It was almost as controversial as *Tobacco Road*, and it was twenty-five years before the book was turned into a movie.

In 1936, he came to Florida with famed photographer Margaret Bourke-White to work on a book documenting the poverty in the South, *You Have Seen Their Faces*. Bourke-White took the pictures while Caldwell wrote accompanying essays. One trip took them to Belmont, Florida, near the Georgia border. They captured a picture of a little girl standing beside a

Erskine Caldwell became a sensation with his novel *Tobacco Road. Library of Congress.*

child in a rocking chair. The walls are covered with pages of old magazines to keep out the cold weather. The caption reads, "Little brother began shriveling up eleven years ago."

The time they spent together led to marriage, which lasted three years.

Caldwell's work declined and was generally lumped with cheap paperback potboilers. He returned to Florida in the 1970s, then moved to Arizona where he died in 1987.

FRANK SLAUGHTER

Frank Slaughter combined writing and politics to become a leader in both. Despite placing books on the bestseller list and seeing them turned into movies, he remained a mediocre writer and seemed more interested in politics.

Slaughter received his medical degree at the age of twenty-two and moved to Jacksonville to work at the city's Riverside Hospital. He purchased a sixty-dollar typewriter on credit—paying five dollars a month—and began cranking out story after story. Unfortunately, no one wanted his stories. In five years, he sold just one story, earning twelve dollars.

When Pulitzer Prize–winning author Marjorie Kinnan Rawlings was admitted to the hospital, Slaughter saw his chance and gave her fifteen pages of his writing to read. She read the work and told him to "stick to operating."

Far from being discouraged, he doubled his efforts and wrote a book based loosely on his life, titled *That None Should Die.* It tells the story of a doctor in a southern city who faces the rising tide calling for government control of medicine—socialized medicine.

At first, his effort was no more successful than his articles—six publishers rejected the manuscript. Then, a local librarian read the manuscript, and when a salesman from Doubleday came to sell the library books, she showed it to him. The salesman passed it along to an editor who liked the story but not Slaughter's writing. A series of rewrites followed, and when it was finally published it made the bestseller list. Many of the sales were to physicians who shared his political views; some purchased multiple copies to give to patients.

Frank Slaughter became a bestselling author thanks to his use of ghost writers. *Florida Archives.*

That established a pattern: Slaughter was good at coming up with plots but miserable at writing. The 1941 book made him a leader in the medical community, and he became a spokesman for the campaign against socialized medicine.

At the end of World War II, the calls for socialized medicine grew louder, and Slaughter became involved in politics. In 1950, Florida senator Claude Pepper, the leading supporter of socialized medicine, was up for reelection, and Slaughter organized physicians throughout the state to defeat him. He urged physicians to call their patients and urge them to vote against Pepper. Pepper lost.

Slaughter wrote more than forty novels—the last in 1987—and each one sold more than one million copies. His eye for detail was amazing and his storylines riveting, but even Slaughter admitted he was not a very good writer.

William DuBois was given credit for "helping" write twenty-seven of Slaughter's books. DuBois was the editor of the *New York Times Book Review*, which often reviewed the books written by DuBois, and it was DuBois who placed them on the bestseller list.

Slaughter also wrote some swashbuckling novels under the name C.V. Terry, including *Buccaneer Surgeon* and *Deadly Lady of Madagascar*. The covers usually featured women in various stages of undress and would have shocked his traditional readers and neighbors in conservative Jacksonville.

Several of his books were made into movies, including *Sangaree*, which was filmed in 3D and stars Fernando Lamas as a Revolutionary War doctor. His 1967 book *Doctor's Wives* was filmed twice, and *The Song of Ruth* became *The Story of Ruth*.

Slaughter died in 2001 at the age of ninety-three.

SOUTH FLORIDA

ISAAC BASHEVIS SINGER

In 1948, Isaac Bashevis Singer and his wife boarded a train in New York in the middle of winter for a trip to Miami, their first. He recalled years later, "I could hardly believe my eyes—the water, the buildings, the indescribable glow, and the palm trees. The palm trees especially made an impression on me."

Arriving in Miami, he said, "I had a feeling I had come to paradise."

The couple checked in at the Hotel Pierre, one of the dozens of art deco hotels built in the 1930s. The Pierre was best known for its low prices. "We were young and we had little money and that seemed a bit much, but we got a room that had a balcony. I stood on that balcony and stared at a palm tree for hours and I was happy."

The journey to Miami began more than a decade earlier when Singer emigrated from Poland amid the growing Nazi threat from neighboring Germany. A year earlier, he had published his first novel, *Satan in Goray*. In New York, he went to work for a Yiddish-language newspaper, the *Forward*, and began to build his reputation as a writer.

After the Pierre, he moved to another classic art deco hotel, the Crown, where he wrote his first major novel and the first to be published in English, *The Family Maskatt*. The book traces a Jewish family in Poland from 1911 to 1930, a subject Singer knew well. He also began producing stories set in Miami Beach.

He moved to South Florida permanently in 1973. One of his grandchildren came to visit in 1982 and said her grandfather took her to the block-long "Isaac Bashevis Singer Boulevard."

In 1978, he won the Nobel Prize, further increasing his renown and pushing up sales of his works. For most of his life, he had struggled with money, but now he was making over $500,000 a year. The University of Miami named him a distinguished professor with an attractive salary. He was so successful that for the first time, he had to get an unlisted telephone number.

He was lonely and depressed by his advancing years. At a University of Miami function, someone lightheartedly asked,

Isaac Singer discovered Miami Beach when he was still an unknown writing for a Yiddish publication. *Florida Archives.*

"How does it feel to be seventy-seven years young?" Singer turned angry and said, "Don't ask such questions! No one is years young. A man is years old, and it is not a joke. It is nothing to joke about. It is a terrible thing to be old, not a joke."

His personal life had always been something of a mess. He left behind a common-law wife in Poland and remarried but was involved with other women in Miami. He broke with his longtime mistress and ended another relationship with his secretary. His relationship with his wife, Alma, was strained. Sometimes he would embarrass her in public, and other times he would praise her, as he did in 1982. "My wife is a saint. For the 42 years of our marriage she had to put up with a lot of nonsense, including supporting my writing as a buyer for department stores in the days when one article for the Jewish daily, *Forward*, earned $25. Alma is like my Rock of Ages."

By the late 1980s, his health was failing. He suffered from Alzheimer's disease and often could not recognize longtime friends. It was a strange type of Alzheimer's. He could go all day without recognizing family members and then say, "I certainly am the greatest Yiddish writer living."

He moved to a nursing home and died in 1991.

ELMORE LEONARD

Elmore Leonard came to Florida with his literary reputation already established, but like many authors, he found in Florida limitless ideas. Leonard was born in New Orleans but grew up in Detroit, where his father worked for General Motors. He served in World War II, then took a job with an advertising agency while finishing college.

At the University of Detroit, he began writing articles and sending them to magazines. In 1951, he sold his first article to *Argosy*, a men's magazine. Five of his stories were made into movies, including *3:10 to Yuma* and *Joe Kidd*. They attracted major stars such as Paul Newman, Clint Eastwood and Burt Lancaster. In all, nineteen of his books and short stories were turned into movies.

In 1985, his novel *Glitz* was such a success it enabled him to buy homes in North Pompano Beach and North Palm Beach. In Florida, he found sunshine and ideas for some of his best-known books.

His first novel with a Florida connection was *Gold Coast* in 1980, the story of a mob wife trying to evade her late husband's last wishes. Other Florida-based books followed, including one of his best known, *Get Shorty*, which became a movie starring John Travolta and Gene Hackman. Eight of his thirty-two books are set in Florida. *La Brava*, considered one of his best, is about a former movie queen whose career had soared and faded. The book contains scenes in a Delray Beach mental facility.

He bought his mother a small motel near the ocean in Pompano Beach, and his 1982 book *Cat Chase*, features a character who runs a motel in Pompano Beach.

His books are populated with gangsters, loan sharks and other characters, many of whom Leonard knew.

He died in 2013 after redefining the crime thriller and setting the pace for other Florida writers who would also focus on the state's underbelly and quirks.

Elmore Leonard is one of the many writers drawn to the Key West Literary Seminar. *Courtesy Key West Literary Seminar.*

JAMES PATTERSON

James Patterson was already a success when he began writing books and was already world-famous when he moved to Florida. He was an advertising director at J. Walter Thompson, the giant agency, when he wrote his first book. It sold about ten thousand copies, a respectable if not impressive number for a first novel.

It was enough to lead him to quit his job to devote himself to writing.

His first book, *The Thomas Berryman Number*, received an Edgar Award.

His 1993 book *Along Came a Spider* seemed an unlikely blockbuster. It deals with an African American detective who has a doctorate from Johns Hopkins and is raising two children after his wife is killed in a drive-by shooting. Patterson convinced his publisher, Little Brown, to try television advertising to promote the book, and it quickly became a bestseller.

From there, his career zoomed, with bestsellers coming at a record pace. He created The Women's Murder Club series, which brought him more fans, then moved into other genres with *Miracle on the 17th Green* in 1996. The same year, he published two more bestsellers: *Jack and Jill* and *Hide and Seek*. Patterson's publishers worried that his fans could not digest his high output, but he proved them wrong. He hired a group of writers to help him write his books, increasing his output even more.

He has sold more than 400 million books and will surely pass half a billion before he puts down his pen.

His success as a writer brought him to Florida, where he purchased an eleven-thousand-square-foot Palm Beach mansion on the Intracoastal Waterway for $5.2 million in 1999, then sold it and purchased a twenty-one-thousand-square-foot estate on two acres on the ocean.

One publication estimated that his books bring him $80 million a year. They also brought him a National Humanities Medal in 2019.

In Florida, he plunged into local charitable causes, raising money for literacy projects and supporting law enforcement. He has established a scholarship fund at Florida Atlantic University, given thousands of books to schools and made appearances at schools to encourage reading. He also raised $170,000 at the Palm Beach Policeman's Ball. One man bid $50,000 to have a character in one of Patterson's books named for his daughter. By selling the names of his characters, he has raised more than $1 million for charity. In addition, he teamed up with Miami Heat star Dwayne Wade to promote literacy and reading and has sponsored newspaper advertisements to encourage reading.

Patterson seems driven to prove that he can be a success no matter what the genre. He has written mysteries, thrillers, science fiction, fantasy, romance, graphic novels and even a nonfiction book about Tourette syndrome.

BIBLIOGRAPHY

Bartram, William, and Mark Van Doren. *Travels of William Bartram*. Mineola, NY: Dover Publications, 1955.

Beach, Rex. *Personal Exposures*. New York: Harper & Brothers, 1943.

Bellman, Samuel Irving. *Marjorie Kinnan Rawlings*. Woodbridge, CT: Twayne, 1974.

Bishop, Morris. *The Odyssey of Cabeza Da Vaca*. Westport, CT: Greenwood Press, 1971.

Blume, Judy. *Are You There God? It's Me, Margaret*. New York: Atheneum, 2005.

Breslin, Jimmy. *Damon Runyan: A Life*. New York: Ticknor & Fields, 1992.

Brown, Loren G. *Totch: A Life in the Everglades*. Gainesville: University Press of Florida, 2018.

Buffett, Jimmy. *A Pirate Looks at Fifty*. New York: Ballantine Books, 2000.

———. *Tales from Margaritaville*. New York: Mariner Books, 2002.

Buntline, Ned. *Matanzas, or, A Brothers Revenge: A Tale of Florida*. Boston: George R. Williams, 1970.

———. *The White Wizard: Or, The Great Prophet of the Seminoles*. New York: Beadle & Adams, 1879.

Cabot, Meg. *The Princess Diaries*. New York: HarperCollins Publishers, 2020.

Caldwell, Erskine. *Tobacco Road and God's Little Acre*. New York: Nelson Doubleday Inc., 1985.

———. *You Have Seen Their Faces*. Athens: University of Georgia Press, 2018.

Carr, Virginia Spencer, and Donald Pizer. *Dos Passos: A Life*. Evanston, IL: Northwestern University Press, 2004.

Carson, Rachel. *Silent Spring*. Boston: Houghton Mifflin, 1962.

Castellanos, Juan de, and Babín María Teresa. *Elegía De Varones Ilustres De Indias De Juan De Castellanos: Elegía VI (A La Muerte De Juan Ponce De León, Donde Se Cuenta La Conquista Del Boriquén Con Otras Muchas Particularidades)*. San Juan: Estado Libre Asociado De Puerto Rico, Editorial Del Departamento De Instrucción Pública, 1967.

Chambers, E.K. *Samuel Taylor Coleridge: A Biographical Study*. Westport, CT: Greenwood Press, 1978.

Clark, James C. *Pineapple Anthology of Florida Writers*. Sarasota, FL: Pineapple Press Inc., 2013.

Clark, Tom. *Jack Kerouac: A Biography*. New York: Thunder's Mouth Press, 2001.

Coleridge, Samuel Taylor, and Frederick H. Sykes. *Rime of the Ancient Mariner*. Durham, NC: Duke Classics, 2020.

Connelly, Michael. *Lincoln Lawyer*. New York: Grand Central, 2020.

Crane, Hart. *The Collected Poems of Hart Crane*. New York: Liveright Publishing Corporation, 1946.

Crane, Stephen, and R.W. Stallman. *Stephen Crane: An Omnibus*. New York: Alfred A. Knopf, 1976.

Crews, Harry. *The Hawk Is Dying*. New York: Knopf, 1973.

Crews, Harry, and Tobias Wolff. *A Childhood, the Biography of a Place*. New York: Penguin Books, 2022.

Davis, Linda H. *Badge of Courage: The Life of Stephen Crane*. Boston: Houghton Mifflin, 1998.

Devlin, James E. *Elmore Leonard*. Westport, CT: Twayne, 1999.

———. *Erskine Caldwell*. Westport, CT: Twayne, 1984.

Dickinson, Jonathan, et al. *Journal, or, Gods Protecting Providence: Being the Narrative of a Journey from Port Royal in Jamaica to Philadelphia between August 23, 1696 and April 1, 1697*. New Haven, CT: Yale University Press, 1961.

Dillard, Annie. *Pilgrim at Tinker Creek*. New York: Harper Perennial, 2016.

Dorsey, Tim. *Atomic Lobster*. New York: HarperCollins, 2009.

———. *Florida Roadkill*. New York: William Murrow, 2018.

Douglas, Marjory Stoneman. *Everglades: River of Grass*. Sarasota, FL: Pineapple Press, 2021.

Douglas, Marjory Stoneman, and John Rothchild. *Marjory Stoneman Douglas: Voice of the River*. Sarasota, FL: Pineapple Press, 2011.

Edel, Leon. *Henry James: A Life*. New York: HarperCollins, 1987.

Fitzgerald, F. Scott. *Tender Is the Night*. New York: Penguin Books, 2019.

Fitzgerald, F. Scott, and Malcolm Cowley. *The Stories of F. Scott Fitzgerald: A Selection of 28 Stories*. New York: Charles Scribner's Sons, 2011.

Frank, Pat. *Alas, Babylon*. New York: Harper Perennial/Olive Editions, 2015.

Goldsmith, Oliver, et al. *The Deserted Village: A Poem Written by Oliver Goldsmith and Illustrated by Edwin A. Abbey, R.A.* New York: Harper & Brothers, 1902.

Hadda, Janet. *Isaac Bashevis Singer: A Life*. Madison: University of Wisconsin Press, 2003.

Hiaasen, Carl. *Team Rodent: How Disney Devours the World*. New York: Random House Publishing Group, 2010.

———. *Tourist Season*. New York: Berkley, 2016.

Hiaasen, Carl, and Diane Stevenson. *Paradise Screwed: Selected Columns of Carl Hiaasen*. Gainesville: University Press of Florida, 2009.

Holmes, Oliver Wendell. *The Poetical Works of Oliver Wendell Holmes*. New York: Houghton, Mifflin and Company, 1893.

Howells, William Dean. *Confession of St. Augustine*. New York: Outlook, 2020.

Hurston, Zora Neale. *Their Eyes Were Watching God*. New York: HarperLuxe, 2008.

Irmscher, Christoph. *John James Audubon: Writings and Drawings*. New York: Library of America, 1999.

Jackson, Carlton. *Zane Grey*. Westport, CT: Twayne, 1989.

James, Henry. *The American Scene*. New York: Penguin Classics, 2018.

Johnson, James Weldon. *The Autobiography of an Ex-Coloured Man*. New York: Hill and Wang, 1995.

Kantor, MacKinlay. *Andersonville*. New York: Penguin, 2016.

Kaufelt, Lynn Mitsuko. *Key West Writers and Their Houses*. Sarasota, FL: Pineapple Press, 1991.

Kennedy, John F. *Profiles in Courage*. New York: Harper, 1964.

Kerouac, Jack. *On the Road*. New York: Viking Press, 1957.

Kerouac, John. *The Dharma Bums*. New York: Viking Press, 1958.

Kerstein, Robert J. *Key West on the Edge: Inventing the Conch Republic*. Gainesville: University Press of Florida, 2012.

Lanier, Sidney. *Florida: Its Scenery, Climate, and History: with an Account of Charleston, Savannah, Augusta, and Aiken: a Chapter for Consumptives; Various Papers on Fruit-Culture: and a Complete Hand-Book and Guide*. Philadelphia: J.B. Lippincott & Co., 1876.

Lanier, Sidney, and Henry Wysham Lanier. *Letters of Sidney Lanier: Selections from His Correspondence, 1866–1881, with Portraits*. Freeport, NY: Books for Libraries Press, 1972.

Leonard, Elmore. *Glitz*. New York: Harper, 2011.

Levy, Eugene. *James Weldon Johnson: Black Leader, Black Voice*. Chicago: University of Chicago Press, 1973.

Ludington, Townsend. *Twentieth Century Odyssey: The Life of John Dos Passos*. New York: E.P. Dutton, 1980.

MacDonald, John D. *The Deep Blue Good-by*. New York: Gold Medal Books/Fawcett, 1964.

McCarthy, Kevin. *The Book Lovers Guide to Florida: Authors, Books, and Literary Sites*. Sarasota, FL: Pineapple Press, 1992.

McIver, Stuart B. *Hemingway's Key West*. Sarasota, FL: Pineapple Press, 2002.
———. *Touched by the Sun*. Sarasota, FL: Pineapple Press, 2008.

McKeen, William. *Homegrown in Florida*. Gainesville: University Press of Florida, 2012.
———. *Mile Marker Zero: The Moveable Feast of Key West*. Gainesville: University Press of Florida, 2016.

Mencken, Henry L. *Newspaper Days 1899–1906*. New York: Knopf, 1975.

Millay, Edna St. Vincent. *Collected Lyrics of Edna St. Vincent Millay*. New York: Perennial Library, 1990.

Moylan, Virginia Lynn. *Zora Neale Hurston's Final Decade*. Gainesville: University Press of Florida, 2011.

Murphy, George. *The Key West Reader: The Best of Key West's Writers, 1830–1990*. Key West, FL: Tortugas, 1990.

O'Sullivan, Maurice J. *Have You Not Hard of Floryda?: The Origins of American Multiculturalism in Florida's Colonial Literature, 1513–1821*. Cocoa Beach: Florida Historical Society Press, 2019.

O'Sullivan, Maurice J., and Jack C. Lane. *The Florida Reader: Visions of Paradise, from 1530 to the Present*. Sarasota, FL: Pineapple Press, 2010.

Patterson, James. *Along Came a Spider*. New York: Grand Central Publishing, 2018.

Pittman, Craig. *Manatee Insanity: Inside the War over Florida's Most Famous Endangered Species*. Gainesville: University Press of Florida, 2010.
———. *The Scent of Scandal: Greed, Betrayal, and the World's Most Beautiful Orchid*. Gainesville: University Press of Florida, 2014.

Pittman, Craig, and Matthew Waite. *Paving Paradise: Florida's Vanishing Wetlands and the Failure of No Net Loss*. Gainesville: University Press of Florida, 2010.

Pratt, Theodore. *The Barefoot Mailman*. Hobe Sound, FL: Florida Classics Library, 1993
———. *Mr. Limpet*. New York: Alfred A. Knopf, 1945.

Proby, Kathryn Hall, and John James Audubon. *Audubon in Florida*. Coral Gables: University of Miami Press, 1981.

Rawlings, Marjorie Kinnan. *South Moon Under*. New York: Charles Scribner's Sons, 2020.

Rawlings, Marjorie Kinnan, and Edward Shenton. *Cross Creek*. New York: Charles Scribner's Sons, 1942.

Rawlings, Marjorie Kinnan, and Ivan Doig. *The Yearling*. New York: Scribner, an Imprint of Simon & Schuster, Inc., 2021.

Rawlings, Marjorie Kinnan, and Julia Scribner Bigham. *Marjorie Rawlings Reader; Sel. and Ed. with an Introduction by J. S. Bigham*. New York: Charles Scribner's Sons, 1956.

Samuels, Peggy, and Harold Samuels. *Frederic Remington: A Biography*. Austin: University of Texas Press, 1985.

Scott, Phil. *Hemingway's Hurricane: The Great Florida Keys Storm of 1935*. New York: International Marine/McGraw-Hill, 2006.

Singer, Isaac Bashevis. *The Family Moskat*. New York: Farrar, Straus & Giroux, 2007.

Slaughter, Frank G. *That None Should Die*. Garden City, NY: Doubleday and Company, 1941.

Sorensen, Theodore C. *Counselor: A Life at the Edge of History*. New York: Harper Perennial, 2009.

Stevens, Wallace. *The Collected Poems of Wallace Stevens*. New York: Vintage Books, 2015.

Thulesius, Olav. *Harriet Beecher Stowe in Florida, 1867 to 1884*. Jefferson, NC: McFarland & Co., 2001.

Wagenknecht, Edward. *Harriet Beecher Stowe*. New York: Oxford University Press, 1965.

———. *John Greenleaf Whittier: A Portrait in Paradox*. New York: Oxford University Press, 1967.

Walker, Jonathan. *The Branded Hand: Trial and Imprisonment of Jonathan Walker*. New York: Arno Press, 1969.

Whitman, Albery Allson. *The Rape of Florida*. Whitefish, MT: Kessinger Publishing, 2010.

Whitman, Walt. *Walt Whitman: Selected Poems*. New York: Library of America, 2003.

Williams, Blanche Colton. *Great American Short Stories: O. Henry Memorial Prize Winning Stories, 1919–1934*. New York: Doubleday, Doran & Company Inc., 1935.

Yardley, Jonathan. *Ring: A Biography of Ring Lardner*. Lanham, MD: Rowman & Littlefield, 2001.

ABOUT THE AUTHOR

James C. Clark is a senior lecturer at the University of Central Florida. He is the author of ten books on Florida history, including *Florida: A Concise History*, and the editor of a three-volume anthology of Florida literature. He earned his doctorate in Florida history at the University of Florida. His work has been honored by the Florida Historical Society, the Florida Magazine Association and the Florida Society of Newspaper Editors. He lives in Orlando.